DATE DUE

Changing for Good

PRACTICAL STEPS FOR BREAKING
YOUR NEGATIVE PATTERNS

Raymond Causey

To the four people on this planet who make my life sweet:
Kimya Joi Causey, my first-born and future broadcast journalist.
(Kimya, the sky is the limit for you!)
Whitney Rae Causey, my gifted one. (Whit, always remember—you have a little extra!)
Brian Jamal Causey, my sleeping giant. (God is going to use you, Brian!)
Courtney Renae' Causey, my "baby girl" and special little friend. (Always stay as you are, Court.)
And to Donna, my wife, mother of our children and my "anchor"—
you are an incredible woman, your godly influence has truly helped to change my life for good!

InterVarsity Press
P.O. Box 1400, Downers Grove, IL 60515-1426
World Wide Web: www.ivpress.com
E-mail: mail@ivpress.com

©*2002 by Raymond Causey*

InterVarsity Press® is the book-publishing division of InterVarsity Christian Fellowship/USA®, a student movement active on campus at hundreds of universities, colleges and schools of nursing in the United States of America, and a member movement of the International Fellowship of Evangelical Students. For information about local and regional activities, write Public Relations Dept., InterVarsity Christian Fellowship/USA, 6400 Schroeder Rd., P.O. Box 7895, Madison, WI 53707-7895, or visit the IVCF website at <www.ivcf.org>.

All Scripture quotations, unless otherwise indicated, are taken from the New American Standard Bible, © 1960, 1962, 1963, 1971, 1972, 1973, 1975, 1977 by the Lockman Foundation. Used by permission.

Cover design: Cindy Kiple; cover image: Getty Images

ISBN 0-8308-2307-7

Printed in the United States of America ∞

Library of Congress Cataloging-in-Publication Data

Causey, Raymond, 1955-
  Changing for good: practical steps for breaking your negative patterns/Raymond Causey.
    p. cm.
Includes bibliographical references.
  ISBN 0-8308-2307-7 (pbk.: alk. paper)
  1. Christian life. 2. Change (Psychology)—Religious aspects—Christianity. I. Title.
   BV4509.5.C38 2002
   248.4—dc21
                                                                          2002004048

| P | 17 | 16 | 15 | 14 | 13 | 12 | 11 | 10 | 9 | 8 | 7 | 6 | 5 | 4 | 3 | 2 | 1 |
| Y | 16 | 15 | 14 | 13 | 12 | 11 | 10 | 09 | 08 | 07 | 06 | 05 | 04 | 03 | 02 |

CONTENTS

1 || Making Right Choices

The shrill ring of the telephone shattered the tranquility of a deep sleep. For several long moments I lay in my bed unable to determine if I was awake or having a terrible dream. I glanced at the clock on the nightstand; it was 2:00 a.m. I sighed as I reached for the phone, "Oh Lord, let all be well."

The voice at the other end of the telephone was familiar, but the words cut like a dagger. "Raymond, someone killed Tommy." As I lay there stunned by what I had heard, I pictured Tommy's tall, muscular body slumped over in some dark alley or on the cold pavement of some deserted street. No longer tall, no longer strong, just lying . . . lifelessly. There was nothing I could do. There were no words. I just lay in my bed confronted with the numbing fact that a member of my family was gone.

Tommy was the second son of my older sister. He was killed just one day before his twenty-third birthday as he and a friend attempted to rob a local tavern. Many believed that Tommy got just what he deserved. But having known Tommy from the time of his birth and seeing his potential, I viewed his death as a tragic loss.

Tommy was not a "bad" person. In fact there was a lot of good in him. He was a sensitive young man who seemed on the verge of turning his life around. But being a good person does not mean that you will always make the right choices in life. On a cold December night, Tommy made a very bad decision. Unfortunately the price he paid for that decision cost him the most precious thing he had: his life.

THE HIGH COST OF DECISIONS

Most of us will not end up like Tommy did, lying face down with a bullet lodged in his back. But I wonder, what price are you paying for a poor decision that you have made? Do you feel trapped in a bad marriage as a result of a poor choice? Are you hopelessly hooked on drugs due to a dreadful decision? Are you laboring under the weight of guilt and shame because as a young teen you decided to have an abortion? In what private hell are you living each day? In what ways have your decisions negatively affected your life?

Contrary to what our culture tells us, I believe there is a tremendous price tag attached to the decisions we make. In my own life, I sometimes wonder how things would be if I had made different choices in certain areas. For instance, as a high school student, I should have excelled academically. The courses I took were not at all difficult. In fact many of my classes seemed too easy. However, I graduated at the bottom of my class. I failed as a student not because I was unable to do the work but because I *made a decision* to do only enough to get by.

Unfortunately my poor attitude and lack of motivation cost me a college athletic scholarship. Eventually I did go to college—with a new attitude. But several years had elapsed, and I was nearly thirty when I finally graduated.

DECISIONS THAT SHAPE OUR LIVES

More than anything, your decisions determine the degree of change that you will experience in your life. If you are struggling with a bad attitude, in order to overcome that problem you must make a decision to do something about it. If anger has you in its grip, you must realize that the pathway to deliverance begins with a decision to change. If your desire is to learn more about the Bible, then you must choose to spend more time in Bible study and prayer.

It is in the moments of decision that you set into motion the events and circumstances that define your life. When I look at you, I see more than the shape of your face, the color of your eyes or the size of your nose. Sure, I notice those things. But your appearance is only a small part of who you are. There is much more.

When I look at you, I also see a history of choices and decisions that you have made. To a large extent, these choices and decisions are responsible for creating your present reality and bringing you to the place you are today. Of course I am not saying that a person's choices are the only factors involved in determining who they are or what they become. There are other things to consider. What I am suggesting, however, is that our choices and decisions play a significant role in shaping our lives.

Dr. Ben Carson, the brilliant African American surgeon and author of the book *Gifted Hands,* talks about his inner struggle with anger and the crucial decision that turned his life around. As a youth, Carson waged a fierce battle to control his temper. Several times his short fuse led him to the edge of disaster.

One day after a particularly nasty flare up (he nearly stabbed a friend to death), he decided to do something about his problem. In desperation Carson went into his small bathroom, closed the door and wrestled with God about his temper. After several hours, with tears streaming down his face, he asked God to take away the anger. And God did. Young Ben Carson emerged from that room a changed person.

Carson went on to become a skilled surgeon and gained worldwide recognition for his part in the first successful separation of Siamese twins who were joined at the back of the head. Overcoming anger was a turning point in Carson's life. But understand that his deliverance from anger did not happen by chance. It happened by choice! Ben Carson made a decision to change by turning to God instead of surrendering to the tyranny of a destructive personality trait.[1]

Unlike Ben Carson, I am afraid, far too many of us drift through life on the winds of chance. We deceive ourselves into believing that things will eventually fall into place by themselves. Or we foolishly hope that the issues in our lives will mysteriously disappear on their own.

Rather than being proactive and turning to God, we often surrender to the very circumstances or challenges that rob us of joy and take away the excitement of living. Let there be no mistake, transformation will not take place apart from a decision. God often initiates the process of change in our lives at the point of a decision that we make!

But let's face it, making the hard decisions, especially when those decisions call for personal change, is not always simple. In fact choosing what is right for our lives, at times, can be quite difficult. For most of us, it is far easier to passively accept mediocrity than to intentionally pursue excellence. Why is this so?

One reason has to do with external forces that condition us, dictating our choices and to some extent determining our destiny. These factors, such as experience, environment, genetics or education, can greatly impact human motivation and behavior.

While there is a degree of validity in citing the external forces that influence our behavior, I believe the real issue for the majority of people has more to do with the internal forces that influence our wills.

In this book I want to expose the spiritual dynamics that are at work behind the scenes, influencing our wills and hindering our ability to consistently make godly choices. There are two extremely powerful forces that often sabotage our desire and determination to obey God: the *subtlety of sin* and the *power of perspective*. Although other forces also come into play, I believe that these two are most dangerous in leading us down a path of self-destruction. Bringing these dark forces into the light is our first step toward changing for good.

2 || It's Not My Fault!

The grisly slayings of José and Kitty Menendez sent shock waves of disbelief through the affluent suburb of Los Angeles. On August 20, 1989, the night of the killing, Lyle and Eric Menendez burst into the family room of their wealthy parents' Bel Air mansion, put shotguns to their parents' heads and emptied more than fifteen rounds.

When the Menendez brothers were arrested seven months later, they showed little remorse for their actions; instead they felt justified in what they did. The brothers insisted that they were severely mistreated as children, and the many years of physical, sexual and emotional abuse by their parents pushed them over the edge. The defense attorneys agreed, suggesting that the real victims in this case were not the murdered parents but Lyle and Eric Menendez.[1]

The drama and celebrity surrounding the Menendez trial exposed the misguided priorities of two young men who, despite wealth and privilege, found themselves trapped inside a tangled web of fear, greed, deception and murder. The defense strategy of the attorneys, along with the finger pointing by the brothers during the trial, revealed a far more pervasive problem in our society: the problem of blame-shifting.

Blame-shifting is the reluctance or refusal to take responsibility for our life choices or circumstances. It is the voice of a skewed conscience that shouts in the face of guilt, emotional pain, failure or the consequences of a poor choice: "It's not my fault!"

Lyle and Eric Menendez's "shout" was loud and clear. Their effort to absolve themselves of murder by impugning the character and reputation of their parents is a classic example of blame-shifting. And while I do not expect that any of us will end up in a court of law facing double homicide charges, I am convinced that we often find ourselves imprisoned in a life of defeat simply because we have cultivated the habit of blaming others for our problems.

A ROADBLOCK TO CHANGE

We engage in the destructive behavior of blame-shifting for a variety of reasons. At times we do it to avoid embarrassment. Other times we pass the buck because of fear or in order to keep our "respectable" reputations or careers intact. Former president Bill Clinton's attempt to escape the consequences of his inappropriate conduct is a good example of this type of blame-shifting. By uttering the words, "I did not have sex with that woman, Miss Lewinsky,"[2] Clinton not only deceived our nation, he also communicated a message that lying, rationalizing and justifying wrong behavior is acceptable as long as you can get away with it.

Of course the irony is that we do not get away with anything! When we think we have successfully escaped detection or the consequences of a poor choice as a result of blame-shifting, in reality we only tighten the noose of dysfunction around our own necks. That is why it is crucial to understand that blame-shifting is a major roadblock in the process that leads to personal transformation. Each time we rationalize wrong behavior or make excuses for poor choices, we reinforce a negative pattern that makes it easier to repeat the dysfunctional behavior in the future.

Negative patterns in our lives are impossible to break if we refuse to take ownership of them. Choosing to own our pain, our past, our disappointment or dysfunction, and being willing to take the steps necessary to work through those issues is fundamental to experiencing change. No matter how poor the choice or how painful the consequences, at some point we must acknowledge our current circumstances and then pursue a course of action that leads to healing, restoration or recovery.

IT'S YOUR FAULT GOD!

Blame-shifting is common in our culture, but it did not originate with this generation. The reluctance to take responsibility for our choices is a sinful trait that we all inherited from our father Adam. Remember when God asked Adam, "Have you eaten from the tree of which I commanded you not to eat?" What was Adam's response? "The woman whom Thou gavest to be with me, she gave me from the tree, and I ate" (Genesis 3:11-12).

In other words Adam was saying, "It's not my fault. If *you* had not created this woman, I would not be in this predicament. I am not responsible!" Talk about waffling. In his attempt to exonerate himself and escape the consequences of his disobedience, Adam not only pointed the finger of blame at Eve, he also implicated God!

Now before we condemn Adam for his outrageous accusation against God, I suggest we each take a careful look at our own life. Has there ever been a time when you pointed the finger of blame at God? Perhaps you made a bad decision that destroyed your marriage or a poor choice that ruined your credibility on the job. And now in the midst of your frustration or loneliness, you blame God. Perhaps you suffered a terrible injustice, and in your heart you feel that God is at fault for allowing it to happen.

Is there a secret place in your soul to which you retreat and accuse God for the problems or disappointments in your life? Take a moment to think about this. As you reflect, understand that the powerful influence of sin in the heart can make it difficult to detect the problem of blame-shifting, especially when your finger is pointed in the direction of God.

In the Gospel of John we read that a godly woman named Martha pointed the finger of blame at God for the deep personal grief she experienced as a result of her brother Lazarus's death. Martha said to Jesus, "Lord, if You had been here, my brother would not have died" (John 11:21). Without realizing it, Martha—a disciple of Christ—made the Lord the scapegoat for the problem in her life. Did Martha love the Lord? Yes! Was she a follower of Christ's teachings? Absolutely! Yet in Martha's moment of pain, she concluded that Jesus himself was responsible for her misery.

Much like Martha, it is common for us to justify certain behavior or rationalize certain attitudes, feelings and responses to life by saying things like "God, if You had simply done this or that, then I would not be the way I am," or " . . . then I would not have been forced to make such a bad decision." Although common, this type of faulty reasoning is quite dangerous. Not only does it destroy our confidence in God, it also casts a distorted perception in our minds concerning the character and motives of God.

God is not the source of our problems but the solution. Martha eventually came to this realization as she continued her dialogue with Jesus. Although Martha initially blamed the Lord for her broken heart, she soon discovered the wonderful truth that God was the healer of broken hearts. He was not out to hurt her but had come to help her. Upon embracing this truth, Martha put herself in a position to receive from Christ. As a result Jesus changed her life and circumstances by miraculously raising Lazarus from the dead, thus demonstrating his power and confirming that he indeed was Lord (John 11:22-44)!

What about you? Do you blame God for your addiction because as a child God allowed alcoholic parents to raise you? Are feelings of insecurity and low self-esteem producing a pattern of poor choices in your life? Do you blame God for not making you smart enough, tall enough, big enough, thin enough or good enough? Perhaps you blame God for your financial misfortune. Or like Martha, you are blaming God for the emotional grief and loneliness you feel due to the death of a loved one.

Whatever your situation, if your finger is pointed at God it is because you have reached the erroneous conclusion that God is responsible for your disappointment, frustration or misery. As did Martha, you must understand that God is not the source of your problems; he is the solution to them. In the same way that Jesus changed Martha's life and circumstances by raising her brother from the dead, God is able to resurrect hope, healing and purpose in your life when you choose to trust him as opposed to blaming him.

CONSPIRACY?

Colin Ferguson, a Jamaican immigrant, did not blame God for his problems; instead he vented his frustrations out on innocent people whom he considered to be involved in a racist conspiracy to keep him down. On a cold December morning in 1993, armed with a nine-millimeter Ruger semi-automatic handgun,

Ferguson arbitrarily opened fire on a crowded New York/Long Island commuter train. For several terror-filled moments, passengers watched in horror and disbelief as Ferguson, in a deranged fit of rage, unleashed his lethal wrath. When the smoke cleared, six people lay dead and nineteen wounded—some critically.

Disarmed and pinned to the floor, Ferguson showed no remorse for his actions. At the trial, despite a trainload of eyewitnesses, Ferguson refused to accept responsibility for his deadly outburst. Instead Ferguson suggested that a mysterious gunman did the shooting. In the mind of Colin Ferguson, racism and discrimination pushed him beyond the dark edges of his sanity, forcing him to explode.[3] In reality Colin Ferguson was just another sad and tragic story of a blame-shifter who screamed in his heart, "It's not my fault!"

JUST TELL THE TRUTH

At an early age, we learn to point the finger of blame at others for our problems. I detected this tendency in my own kids almost from the time of infancy. As much as I love Kimya, Whitney, Brian and Courtney, it did not take long for me to see that they were a bunch of little sinners! What's more, even when caught red-handed doing something wrong, their first reaction was seldom confession and repentance. Instead they made excuses, rationalized or outright lied in an attempt to escape the consequences of their actions.

One night Donna and I returned home from a speaking engagement. After thanking the sitter for watching our four little ones, Donna disappeared into the kids' bathroom. The tone of her voice when she yelled "Kimya!" and the look on her face when she stormed out of the bathroom let me know that I was in for a long night. The problem? Someone had scribbled with red crayon on the bathroom walls.

This was unacceptable. In an attempt to get to the bottom of it all, we called the kids together in the living room and asked the question: "Who did it?" It was amazing; no one knew anything about the red graffiti on the walls. Apparently it just appeared mysteriously on its own.

On careful investigation, we concluded that our second child, Whitney, was the culprit. I took her to my bedroom and encouraged her to tell the truth. She lied. Not just once but each time I asked the question. Whitney insisted that she was innocent and that it was not her fault. After about forty-five minutes of relentless interrogation on my part and sobbing denials from my daughter, the truth came out. Whitney broke down and confessed.

When the dust settled, I took my little girl in my arms and explained to her the importance of telling the truth. I assured her that I loved her and nothing could change that fact. I also explained that when we blow it, as we all will occasionally, the right thing to do is admit the failure, seek forgiveness and grow from the experience. Whitney got the message.

Whitney was only five years old when this occurred, but I am amazed at the number of adults I counsel who are just as stubborn and unwilling to admit when they are wrong. It may be in their marriage, on the job or even in Christian service. The truth is that we often find it difficult to say, "It's my fault," or "I'm responsible." It is so much easier to shift the blame elsewhere.

REDEFINING BIBLICAL VALUES

Unfortunately we live in a society that contributes to the problem of blame-shifting. Social experts make it very easy for us to justify sinful attitudes and actions by creating the perception that certain behavior is more the result of genetics or environment and not choice. For instance, in the Bible drunkenness is a moral issue that reveals a serious character flaw. In our culture, however, many secular researchers who do not acknowledge the spiritual roots of addiction say that drunkenness is a "disease" that could happen to just about anyone. The implication is that individuals who have a genetic predisposition to alcoholism and other addictions do not have a choice in the matter, or at least they are not responsible for the choices that lead to their condition of addiction.

I disagree. While I acknowledge that certain people may have a predisposition toward addictive behavior, I don't believe that a predisposition in itself is equivalent to a disease, or that it necessarily predetermines choices. On the contrary, the Bible teaches that when we choose habitual sin, the inevitable result or consequence of that choice is bondage or slavery to that sin. In other words, the process leading to addiction starts with a decision—a moral choice—even for those with a genetic predisposition.[4]

Another way that the culture contributes to the problem of blame-shifting is by challenging, rejecting and ultimately redefining biblical values and standards. It is one thing to have a sense of remorse or guilt as a result of knowing that God's Word has been violated. But when we perceive something that is sinful in God's eyes to be acceptable in our own or in the eyes of society, it is difficult for us to recognize (let alone admit) fault or failure.

Take the issue of pride. In the Bible, pride is described as a sinful character trait that leads us down a pathway of destruction. Yet in our culture, not only do we applaud this characteristic in a person, but we also promote and reward it. Most people in our society view independence and self-reliance as a sign of success and not a problem with pride!

The widespread tolerance of immorality is another indication of how the culture has effectively redefined biblical values, thus creating a perception that obscenity, perversion and a host of other illicit sexual activity is acceptable as long as the activity is consensual. It is obvious, in view of the promiscuity in this society, that the stigma of sin no longer serves as a deterrent to immoral behavior. The result is that the disgrace once associated with moral failure has vanished. The shame of adultery is replaced by the tolerance of "affairs." Homosexuals are now "gay," and the abortion of thousands of unborn babies each year is promoted as "pro-choice."

What is the message in all this? It is clear. We live in a society that demands moral freedom apart from moral responsibility. Yet we cannot legitimately practice moral freedom, which is seen in the choices we make, independent of the consequences that are attached to those choices.

David, the anointed king of Israel, learned this lesson the hard way. Even though he was a man after God's own heart, there was a period in David's life when he was driven by the insatiable lust to sleep with another man's wife. Instead of nipping his immoral thoughts in the bud, David toyed with the idea of having sex with Bathsheba until he eventually acted out his fantasy. When Bathsheba became pregnant as a result of their adulterous affair, David attempted to shift the blame to Uriah, Bathsheba's innocent husband. The king did this by calling Uriah from the battlefield and enticing him to sleep with his wife. When Uriah refused, David secretly conspired to kill him in order to conceal his own treachery, and he married Uriah's widow (2 Samuel 11:2-17).

David eventually took full responsibility for his actions and admitted that he was wrong (Psalm 51). However, the consequences of David's scandalous, immoral choices haunted him for the rest of his life. Not only did the child from his union with

Bathsheba die, but the curse of domestic violence, political conspiracy and the threat of military coup hovered like a dark cloud over David's kingdom until the day he died.

Just as King David had to own up to the consequences of his choices, we too must own up to ours. A few years ago I had the task of overseeing the planning, marketing and promotion of an important conference in a major city. I had a team of people working with me to help pull it off. The team was comprised mainly of local volunteers who depended on my leadership and direction to guide them through the process.

As the director of the ministry, I was working to meet several deadlines. Under this pressure, I found myself spending more time and energy on less important projects that were unrelated to the conference and should have been delegated to a staff member. Consequently I failed to provide the leadership necessary for a successful promotional effort.

As the date for the conference approached, it became clear that things were not coming together. Eventually we had to call off the event, causing the ministry to suffer a substantial financial setback. Having to cancel the conference was disappointing and embarrassing. Initially I became defensive and blamed others for the failure, even though I knew inside that it was really my fault.

Of course the Spirit of God convicted me of this sin, and I had no choice but to admit that I blew it. When I finally shared my guilt with our staff, they were forgiving and extremely gracious toward me. Still, I was bothered. It was just too easy to point the finger of blame at others in an attempt to cover my own mismanagement of priorities. As did David, I had sought to escape the consequences of my actions or, in this case, my failure to act. I was troubled because I was a blame-shifter.

What about you? Do you have a dark cloud of consequences

hanging over your life and circumstances? Do you find it difficult to admit when you are wrong? Do you habitually rationalize, justify and excuse your behavior, even when that behavior
is sinful? Is it easy for you to blame others for your faults or failures? If so, then more than likely you, too, are a blame-shifter.
Unless we learn to take responsibility for our choices, actions,
circumstances and consequences, we will never experience freedom from the issues that keep our lives in bondage.

3 || Why Is It So Hard to Do the Right Thing?

The over-stuffed suitcase containing all my worldly possessions rested in the cargo section of the Boeing 747 jetliner. It was January 1978, and I was twenty-two years old. I had lived most of my life in Fort Wayne, Indiana, but things were about to change. On that frigid winter morning, I said goodbye to my parents and boarded a plane headed for the West Coast.

Gazing out of the window as I sat buckled in my seat, I knew that the decision to leave Fort Wayne was the right one. A quiet sense of destiny flooded my heart. Los Angeles, the City of Angels, waited just beyond the horizon. When the plane touched down at LAX (Los Angeles International Airport), I felt like a new man. I was young, I was single, and I was free to live my life as I pleased—that is, until I met Donna.

I met Donna at a little church in Venice, California, that my uncle had invited me to visit. Once there I began to scan the congregation. My eyes landed on Donna. When I saw her, immediately I knew that I was in the right place! Donna was the woman of my dreams.

We wasted little time getting to know each other, and after one year of dating we tied the knot. But married life was not all bliss; the first few years were tough. Of course I loved Donna with all my heart, and she felt the same toward me. However, it only took us a couple of months of living in close proximity to each other to discover that we shared a common trait in our different personalities. We were both sinners! Because this was true, we both had a tendency to be selfish.

Now I know that it is hard to believe that I could be selfish, but it is true. In the early stages of our marriage, I thought it best that the relationship went in one direction—mine! Of course Donna disagreed.

During that period in our relationship, the natural tendency for both Donna and me was to focus on "my rights" and on having things "my way." There were times when we tried to do better. Occasionally we would attempt to alter certain behavior or break negative habits. But the attempts to change only led to frustration and failure. Our marriage was in serious trouble, and we needed something more than good intentions, promises to do better or short-lived adjustments in behavior to save it. What we needed was a fundamental change in our heart attitudes.

As long as Donna and I attempted to fix our problems by treating symptoms (that is, our selfish conduct), we were doomed to react to each other out of habit, thus repeating the same negative behavior that exposed the problems in the first place. Once we realized, however, that selfishness was only an expression of what was in the heart, it became clear what our priority needed to be: to focus less on the symptoms of our problems and more on the root cause.

HEART ATTITUDES

No matter how destructive a particular habit in our lives may be, it is only the tip of the iceberg. The real problem is hidden beneath the surface. It is the attitude of the heart that causes the major damage. Because this is true, in order to experience lasting change in our lives, not only must we deal with bad behavior or habits, we must also deal with the root cause of the behavior and habits.

Just as Donna and I shifted our focus from our actions to our attitudes, you too must move beyond treating the symptoms of your personal struggles and begin addressing the true source of the struggles: your heart attitude.

Whenever we focus solely on changing behavior without considering the cause of that behavior, we run the risk of misunderstanding the full extent of our problem and, more importantly, what it will take to overcome that problem. For this reason, many of us are discouraged by a lack of progress in our lives. It seems that no matter what we do or how hard we try, lasting and significant change is never achieved. Unfortunately we will grow increasingly frustrated until our priority becomes less focused on changing habits and more focused on changing the heart.

Adjusting the heart attitude is not always easy and can often be tricky. This is so because we tend to underestimate the impact of sin in our lives. More than anything else, it is the subtle yet powerful influence of sin in the heart that creates a cesspool of negative patterns in our lives that keeps us stuck in the stagnant waters of mediocrity.

SIN'S IMPACT ON THE HEART

When it comes to gaining insight into the human heart, it is helpful to know what the Bible has to say about its true condition. Inspired by the Spirit of God, the Old Testament prophet Jeremiah flashes the spotlight of truth on the dark side of the heart. What the light reveals is shocking. Jeremiah says: "The heart is more deceitful than all else and is desperately sick; who can understand it?" (Jeremiah 17:9).

Talk about "rotten to the core" . . . the human heart is bad! Although the sentiment of our culture asserts that people are basically good, it is clear from this passage that God disagrees. On the contrary, God's diagnosis of humanity reveals a malignant spiritual tumor that has spread to all aspects of our lives. This spiritual cancer is called *sin,* and it metastasizes from the very center of our being: the heart.

When the Bible talks about sin, it is not so much describing an external action, as it is an internal attitude or condition. In this sense, sin is the lack of moral and spiritual conformity to the will of God. It is this internal failure to conform to the will of God that produces external transgression or violation of the law of God. In a similar sense, when the Bible speaks of the heart it is not a reference to the physical muscle inside the chest which pumps blood through our veins. Rather, it is a word picture that depicts the spiritual, emotional, rational and volitional condition of our being.

In his book *Check Your Character,* Knofel Staton says:

> The heart does not refer to a muscle-center, but to a motivating center that makes the whole man do what he does. It is the source of a person's personality and behavior. It involves a combination of the intellectual, emotional, volitional and spiritual foundations of a person. If these foundations are off or unsettled, then the whole person will be off or unsettled.[1]

When Jeremiah says the heart is deceitful and desperately sick, he is not referring to a physical condition, but a spiritual one. He is saying that sin's impact on the heart has rocked the very foundation of our being, leaving us intellectually, emotionally, volitionally and spiritually unsettled and off base.

Because sin dwells at the motivating center of our being, it has a way of blending in with our personalities and behaviors, making it difficult, if not impossible, to detect its presence and influence.

THE LOG IN MY EYE

As a pastor, I counsel all types of people who have a variety of problems. All too often, the people who come to me are seeking advice about how to deal with a painful issue that is causing misery in their lives. After careful and prayerful probing, we often discover that the true source of their misery is not an external circumstance or another person, but it is an internal attitude or perspective that is rooted in sin. Many times the individual is unaware of their sinful attitude, even though it produces inappropriate responses and wrong choices in the person's life.

On one occasion a woman in the church I used to pastor came to me with complaints about her husband. Within the first few minutes of our conversation, she had meticulously listed all of his mistakes, faults and failures. When I met with the couple, I discovered that much of what this woman had shared about her husband was true. But I also discovered that a major reason why their marriage suffered stemmed from many unresolved issues in this woman's life as well.

While both were quick to point out the failures of their mate, they were blinded to the fact that a root of bitterness in their own hearts contributed to their marital frustration. But therein lies the subtlety of sin. We are astute at finding the faults of others but oblivious to the sin and weaknesses in our own lives. Jesus condemned such spiritual ignorance and self-righteousness in his Sermon on the Mount. Jesus said to the multitude, "And why do you look at the speck that is in your brother's eye but do not notice the log that is in your own eye?" (Matthew 7:3).

The couple in my church is a typical example of this. Each had major issues that were rooted in sin. Yet neither had a clue that their personal sinful attitude was a reason their marriage was crumbling.

It is common for us to dismiss sinful attitudes in our own lives by saying things like "Oh, it's not all that big of a deal," or "That's just the way I am." Such foolish rationalizations only reveal the power of sin and the deceitfulness of our hearts.

WHERE DID IT ALL BEGIN?

To understand the depth to which sin influences the human heart and thus our will to make right choices, we need to journey back to the very beginning. In Genesis the Bible teaches that God created Adam and Eve in his own image.

> Then God said, Let Us make man in Our image, according to Our likeness; and let them rule over the fish of the sea and over the birds of the sky and over the cattle and over all the earth, and over every creeping thing that creeps on the earth. And God created man in His own image, in the image of God He created him; male and female He created them. (Genesis 1:26-27)

Now just stop and think about that for a moment. God created Adam and Eve in his image. The implications of that statement are enormous. I am convinced that we do not fully understand all that being created in the image of God entails. But at least one thing is clear from the passage: God intended for people to be a reflection of himself on planet Earth.

In order to accomplish this divine intention, God originally created Adam and Eve in a state of physical and moral perfection. Both Adam and Eve were awesome specimens of humanity. They enjoyed several advantages that we do not have today. For example, they were physically perfect. For Adam and Eve, there was no need for doctors or medical insurance. No need to swallow a pill to relieve flu symptoms. Sickness, disease and aging were not a part of their reality. There were absolutely no defects or glitches in Adam or Eve. God created them with perfection in mind.

Even more significant was the fact that Adam and Eve were created in a state of moral perfection. This advantage meant that Adam and Eve did not have to struggle with a sinful heart or sin nature. The absence of sin in their hearts enabled our first parents to live in absolute harmony with the goals, objectives and purposes of God. Simply stated, Adam's and Eve's wills were in perfect alignment with the will of God.

WHAT'S INSIDE?

There were no internal dynamics or influences in Adam's and Eve's lives that compelled them to disobey God. In contrast there is a raging conflict that is taking place internally in the life of the believer today. As a result of this internal conflict, Christians find themselves in a daily struggle to consistently do the things that are pleasing to God. The apostle Paul describes this conflict in his letter to the church in Rome:

> For that which I am doing, I do not understand; for I am not practicing what I would like to do, but I am doing the very thing I hate. But if I do the very thing I do not wish to do, I agree with the Law, confessing that it is good. So now, no longer am I the one doing it, but sin that indwells in me. (Romans 7:15-17)

When we give in to temptation, it is usually because our selfish desires have won the battle over our reason in the struggle to influence our wills. Some time ago I made a commitment to spend at least one hour each day in Bible reading, meditation and/or prayer. This has been a wonderful experience for me.

Each day my devotion to Christ grows, and I am learning to walk with him in the details of life.

However there are times when, at the end of an exhausting day, I am tempted to just dive into the sack, pull the covers over my head and say, "Forget the Bible. And prayer? I'll remember to do that while I am dreaming!"

What is interesting is that when I am tempted to forego my commitment to the Lord, I literally feel the tug of war going on between my desire and my reason as they try to persuade my will. My desire says "Dive!" My reason says "Read!" My choice hangs somewhere in the balance of this internal tension.

The truth is that most of life is caught in this tension. But no such tension existed in Adam and Eve; they both were completely free from this internal struggle. As a result they were totally responsive to the will of God, which enabled them to experience deep intimacy with him.

But life in paradise did not last long. Something terrible happened which disrupted Adam and Eve's utopia. What do you suppose it was? You guessed it: *sin.* You see, in addition to being morally and physically perfect, the first humans created were also free moral agents.

FREE AGENTS

Today when we think of free agency, we often associate it with professional sports. For example, in the NBA or NFL a player who is a free agent basically has the freedom to negotiate a contract with any team that is willing to pay his salary. This is a tremendous benefit to the player. It gives him leverage at the bargaining table. As a free agent, he is empowered to make choices, and he is free to determine his own professional destiny.

When God created Adam and Eve, God gave them the power of choice. God equipped them with the liberty and ability to determine their own moral and spiritual destiny, within his sovereign plan and design. God could have created an android or a robot or a person whose programming guaranteed an obedient response. Instead God created two humans with the capacity to act of their own volition or free will.

Adam and Eve were free moral agents. Therefore it was necessary for God to subject them to a moral test of the highest magnitude. This test was designed specifically to try Adam's obedience (and not Eve's), since Adam was the head of the human race. As such, Adam's response to the test would serve to confirm his personal character as well as determine the moral and spiritual condition of the entire human race.

"But why would Adam's character need confirmation?" you may wonder. "Didn't his nature guarantee that he would always do the right thing?" Not necessarily. You see, *nature* and *character* are not synonymous. Our nature has to do with who we are by birth or creation. Our character, on the other hand, has to do with who we become through experience. While it is true that Adam was morally perfect by nature, at the same time, his character had not been tried and tested in the face of opposition. Therefore, while his nature was righteous, his character needed to be confirmed in that righteousness through experience.

Keep in mind that Adam was not born into this world like you and me. He did not experience the natural process of growth, development and maturity like the rest of us. God basically spoke Adam into existence fully grown. While he had the appearance of history, in actuality Adam had no background, frame of reference or experiences of any kind. So although Adam was morally innocent by nature, he needed to prove his character experientially in the face of opposition.

The stage was set. God gave Adam the choice to either give God the right to determine his moral direction and destiny through obedience, or to claim that right for himself through disobedience.

Well, we all know the story. Adam flunked the test. In that moment of failure, he introduced sin into the human race (Romans 5:8). What a dark hour that was. No matter how majestic Adam may have been originally, in that one decisive moment he nullified God's original purpose for his life.

Talk about suffering the consequences of a poor choice . . . the price that Adam paid for that one was devastating. Not only did he lose his innocence, but Adam also lost his intimacy with God. In addition, Adam lost a transparent relationship with Eve. He lost a beautiful home in the garden. He lost authority and dominion over the animal kingdom and the environment. He lost his sense of purpose and significance.

In essence, when Adam fell, he forfeited his divine birthright. Paradise became a jungle, and the presence and power of sin became a dominant, oppressive force in the human experience. Most significant, however, was the fact that when Adam sinned, in that moment, he died.

> And the Lord God commanded the man, saying, "From any tree of the garden you may eat freely; but from the tree of the knowledge of good and evil you shall not eat, for in the day that you eat from it you shall surely die." (Genesis 2:16-17)

On that infamous day in the garden, death visited Adam and Eve. However, the physical manifestation of death did not become a reality for many years. In fact the Bible teaches that Adam lived to the ripe old age of 930. Nevertheless, when Adam sinned, in that very moment he died.

THE SEPARATION OF DEATH

You are probably wondering: "How can the Bible teach that Adam lived to be 930 years old while, at the same time, teaching that he died instantly upon eating from the tree of the knowledge of good and evil?" How do we reconcile what appears to be a contradiction of events in the Garden of Eden?

The solution is simple: we do so by gaining a biblical perspective on the concept of death. When the Bible talks about death, it is not communicating the end of existence; rather it is referring to a separation that occurs. This separation can be applied in three specific ways according to the Bible.

First, there is the separation of the human soul and spirit from the physical body. This is what the Bible refers to as *physical death*. For example, on the day you die (no time soon I trust), your death will not terminate your existence as a person. Of course your physical body will cease to function, but your soul and spirit will continue to exist either in the presence of Christ or in the torment of hell (2 Corinthians 5:8; see also Luke 16:19-31).

Second, the Bible talks about a separation of the human soul and spirit from the life and presence of God. This is known as *spiritual death*. This is the state of all those who have never trusted Jesus Christ as Lord and Savior. Those who are spiritually separated from God are described as being "dead in trespasses and sins" (Ephesians 2:1).

The ultimate separation, according to the Bible, is when the whole person (spirit, soul and resurrected body) is condemned to spend all eternity separated from the life and presence of God in a lake of fire. This separation is called *eternal death* (Revelation 20:14).

When Adam chose to disobey God, the consequences of that decision were not immediate in the sense that he became a physical corpse on the spot or that he and Eve were instantly cast into the lake of fire. It is obvious that this was not the case. The consequences were immediate, however, in that Adam instantly experienced spiritual separation from the life and presence of God.

This spiritual rift between God and Adam jolted Adam's will out of alignment with God's. On that day, Adam became self-willed, and depravity became the spiritual genetic signature of the human heart, thereby destroying our ability to naturally make God-centered choices for our lives.

DEPRAVED PEOPLE

The depravity of humans has been a topic of debate within the Christian community for some time. There are those who believe that depravity is the idea of people not having a moral conscience or sense of right or wrong. Others think that as depraved beings, deep down in the secret places of our hearts we are all diabolical murderers, thieves, drunkards or worse. Is this what the Bible teaches about depravity? Hardly! Depravity does not mean that we are incapable of committing acts of kindness, compassion or other noble deeds of redeeming value. In fact we all probably know someone who does not profess to be a Christian but lives a model life when it comes to being a good, moral person.

On the flip side of the coin, there are people who are typically cruel and dishonest; yet on occasion, when given the right set of circumstances, these mean-spirited souls may commit an act of human kindness. So a casual observation of the human experience shows that the depravity of humanity does not necessarily preclude people from engaging in good deeds.

What *depravity* does mean, however, is that our goodness is insufficient to satisfy the demands of a righteous and holy God.

In God's economy, there are only two moral categories in the universe: good and evil. What separates these two classifications is the absolute holiness of God himself. We may do what appears to be "good" from a human perspective, but when we consider God's absolute holiness, in comparison, all of our "goodness" falls woefully short of God's standard of perfection. It is thereby legitimately categorized by God as evil.

The prophet Isaiah makes the point clear when he writes, "For all of us have become like one who is unclean, and all our righteous deeds are like a filthy garment" (Isaiah 64:6). Centuries later this same truth is echoed by the apostle Paul in his letter to the Romans: "There is none righteous, not even one; there is none who understands, there is none who seeks for God; all have turned aside, together they have become useless; there is none who does good, there is not even one" (Romans 3:10-12).

Depravity, then, is a spiritual condition that renders us incapable of earning favor with God on the basis of human effort. It is a condition of utter corruption and spiritual hopelessness. Depravity is not to be understood in the sense that we are incapable of displaying acts of human kindness. Rather, we are depraved in the sense that in our nature there is a spiritual genetic defect that renders us powerless to perfectly and perpetually make choices that conform to the will of God or that measure up to his standard of righteousness.

Human depravity is not a temporary ailment that passes with time. Instead it is the fundamental condition of the human heart. And it impacts each of us negatively irrespective of our position or status in life.

Adolf Eichmann is recorded in history as one of the worst war criminals the world has ever known. During the Holocaust it is believed that Eichmann personally executed thousands of Jews and presided over the slaughter of millions more. In 1960 Israeli Secret Service agents captured Eichmann in a South American hideout. Eichmann was promptly transported to Israel to stand trial for his atrocities.

During the trial, Yehiel Dinur, a former concentration camp prisoner and survivor of Auschwitz, was called to testify. Upon entering the courtroom Dinur's eyes met the eyes of the man responsible for murdering millions of Jews. As he stared into the face of Eichmann, Yehiel Dinur began to shout and sob, collapsing to the floor. When asked why he broke down, Yehiel Dinur's response was remarkable. "I was afraid about myself," Dinur said. "I saw that I am capable to do this . . . exactly like he."[2]

You see, Adolf Eichmann was not the diabolical monster Dinur had expected. Instead he was an ordinary man, just like anyone else. Indeed depravity is not limited to just a few, but it is the universal condition of the human heart.

SO WHAT?

You may be wondering at this point, "Why should Adam's failure thousands of years ago in some lost paradise affect my ability to make the right choices for my life today?" That, my friend, is a very logical question. It requires, however, a theological response. I will admit that I do not understand all the issues related to this mystery. I do know that the crux of the matter centers on the doctrine of imputation.

The word *imputation* is a legal term. It basically means to charge to one's account. For example, if a wealthy person endorsed a check for one million dollars and deposited it into your savings account as a gift, would that money belong to you? Absolutely! You may not have earned it, but that does not matter. What is important is that the deposit was a legal transaction. Once the one million dollars has been legally transferred into your account, it's yours. You have access to the money just as if

you earned it. That's how imputation works. It is a legal transaction.

But why would God legally transfer Adam's transgression and
depravity to innocent people like you and me? Isn't that unfair?
It certainly seems unfair from a human perspective. However,
God's viewpoint is different from ours. When God created
Adam, he decided to designate him as head of the entire human
race. Theologians refer to this as the federal headship of Adam.
This theological concept basically means that God saw all of hu-
manity potentially and positionally "in" Adam.

As the head of the race, Adam was given authority to act on
behalf of all humanity. As a result of this judicial authority, when
Adam sinned, his transgression became a representative act of
all humanity. God imputed or credited Adam's transgression and
guilt to our spiritual and moral account because, from God's
perspective, Adam was the prototype of the race. As the first,
God allowed Adam to establish the spiritual and moral direction
for all of his descendants to follow. In God's mind, when the prototype of the race failed, all members of the race also failed.
Therefore, when Adam sinned, it was as if we ourselves committed the offense.

My point is this: Adam's failure in the garden fundamentally
altered our nature. Originally the human race, represented by
Adam, had a built-in tendency to respond naturally and instinctively to God. That was our nature. But after the fall, things radically changed for the worse. Depravity invaded our hearts, and
our nature became sinful. Today the human heart is far from being naturally and instinctively responsive to God. It is quite the
opposite; from birth our hearts are naturally and instinctively
rebellious, indifferent and apathetic toward God.

It is precisely due to this sinful heart condition that we struggle so desperately to make right choices for our lives. In our nat-

ural state, we are alienated from God and exist in passive or active rebellion against God. This state of alienation and rebellion emasculates our intellectual, emotional, volitional and spiritual resolve to obey God. It leaves us impotent to make choices that are consistent with God's divine will for our lives.

Our only hope is to be redeemed from the curse of the first Adam by placing our faith in the second Adam: Jesus Christ (Romans 8:1-39; 1 Corinthians 15:45-49). Christ alone is able to give us a new nature and new hearts. Still, once we are redeemed the struggle is not over. The residual effects of depravity and the lingering presence of sin exerts a powerful influence in our lives, making it difficult to consistently choose the way of conformity to the holy character of God.

Now I want you to pause for just a moment and honestly examine your heart. Do you struggle with pride? Are you selfish? Do you have a critical spirit? Are you jealous of others? Do you wrestle with lustful thoughts? Are you lazy? Are you deceitful? Do you nag? Do you eat too much? Do you waste time? Shade the truth? Are you materialistic? Are you fighting an addiction? Are you struggling with homosexuality?

Whatever your personal issue, you must recognize the fact that at the root of the problem is the influence of sin in the heart. Moreover in order to experience lasting change, not only must you deal with negative behavior and habits in your life, but you must also deal with the sinful heart attitude that produces such actions.

A NEW HEART ATTITUDE

Tackling the problem of a sinful heart involves three things. First, we must *acknowledge our condition before God*. The journey that leads to healing and deliverance from the power and dominance of sin begins with a step in the direction of God. God wants to transform our lives, but transformation cannot occur apart from acknowledging our spiritual failure and inadequacy before him.

God already knows our hearts, but he wants us to admit that we have problems that are too big to handle on our own. God is waiting for us to stop denying the reality of sin's power in our lives and over our ability to make right choices. When we do this, we are agreeing with God; and when we agree with God, we put ourselves in a position to be helped by God. Until we acknowledge the presence and power of sin in our hearts, we will continue the practice of sin in our lives.

Second, we must *ask for God's forgiveness and accept God's cleansing.* John the apostle put it this way: "If we say we have no sin, we deceive ourselves, and the truth is not in us. If we confess our sins, He is faithful and righteous to forgive our sins and to cleanse us from all unrighteousness" (1 John 1:8-9). As we have learned, sin and depravity have left a nasty stain on the human heart. The good news is that God is a master heart cleaner! And one of the great truths of Scripture is that God is willing, eager and able to clean our hearts through the forgiveness of sins.

It matters not what offenses we have committed. When we are sincere in seeking God's forgiveness, he is faithful in granting it. However, when God grants forgiveness, it is our responsibility to appropriate his forgiveness by claiming the spiritual cleansing that comes with it. We do this as we choose to forgive ourselves emotionally and psychologically. There is no need for us to cling to the pain of guilt, or to continue in morbid introspection over past failure, when God has thoroughly washed us by the cleansing power of the blood of Jesus Christ.

Finally, we must *take aggressive action against the sin in our lives.* Acknowledging our sins before God, and asking for his forgiveness and cleansing, are necessary steps in overcoming the problems and issues that emerge from out of the dark pit of a sinful heart. Yet, these actions alone are not sufficient to gain total victory. We must take the next step. That step is to declare war on sin. When God reveals sin in our lives, whether it is an attitude, action, thought or habit, we must immediately choose to turn away from the sin and toward God. This response to sin is known as *repentance*.

Repentance is very important. Confession apart from repentance leads only to self-deception and creates a false sense of progress in the quest for change. When we repent, we demonstrate that we are willing to make the hard choices related to our feelings, thoughts and behaviors. These choices ultimately enable us to break the power of negative patterns and put us on a path that leads to change.

A consistent pattern of confession and repentance brings us closer to God. And when we grow closer to God, we gain greater access to his power. Suddenly it is not so hard to do the right thing anymore. With each godly choice, strength is renewed, hope is restored, and we begin to believe that change is possible.

4 || What You See Is Usually What You Get

Choosing the proper perspective in life has a way of keeping us on the right track. But when our perspective and priorities clash with God, the choices we make invariably lead us off course.

HOOP DREAMS

As a kid growing up in the inner city of Fort Wayne, Indiana, I had one goal in mind: to play basketball in the NBA. When my middle school coach tossed me a basketball, he gave me a dream, and I was relentless in my pursuit of that dream.

For many years I poured my life into the game. In the scorching heat, I was out there playing. Rain did not stop me; I still played. In the dead of winter when the courts were frozen over and covered with snow, I simply took my shovel, removed the snow and practiced my jump shot.

I guess you could say I loved the game. I recall my Mom saying many times, "Boy, all you do is eat, drink and sleep basketball!" Mom was right. By the time I reached high school, I had developed into an outstanding basketball player. My reputation grew around the city, coaches were scouting and recruiting me, and I was beginning to think that basketball could be my ticket out of the ghetto.

But something was desperately wrong inside. Even though I was an outstanding basketball player, I was a miserable person. Life was one-dimensional. Everything in my world revolved around basketball. My identity as a person, my self-worth, my sense of significance, my concept of success, my contentment and my sense of purpose were all tied to my performance on that ninety-four-foot hardwood floor.

When I played well, I soared to the heights of self-esteem. On off nights when my "game" was not clicking, I sunk to the depths of depression. Imagine riding that emotional roller coaster as a young person. Although God had other plans for my life, all I could see was basketball. From my perspective the only thing that mattered was scoring points on the court.

Finding ways to score points on the basketball court was easy. Finding my place in life was a totally different ball game. For a long time I was convinced that the NBA was my destiny, but slowly that dream unraveled.

The unraveling began in my senior year of high school when I was declared academically ineligible to finish the basketball season. Flunking off the team was not only an embarrassment to me and to my family, it also significantly reduced my chances of going on to college. Thanks to a couple of coaches I knew, I was able to get into a community college on an athletic scholarship.

Malcolm X Community College was located on the west side of Chicago. It had an outstanding basketball program and was coached by a man who had once played for the Harlem Globetrotters. When I enrolled at Malcolm, I thought my future as a professional athlete was back on track. Unfortunately once again my poor study habits and lack of interest in academics derailed my hopes of moving on. After one season at Malcolm X Community College, I dropped out.

I did not play organized basketball again for three years. That is when I got an opportunity to try out for the NBA at a summer professional league in Los Angeles, California. My coach at the camp was impressed with my talent, but he also knew that I had played only one year of college ball. He tried to convince me to return to school and develop my game. I quickly dismissed his suggestion. In my mind, I was ready to sign a contract.

When the tryouts ended, I was cut from the team. This devastated me. For years I had baffled opponents with slashing moves to the hoop. Now I didn't have a clue what my next move in life would be. I felt paralyzed. I had no way of knowing at the time that four years later I would receive a full scholarship to play basketball for the then-ranked number one NAIA team in the nation, Biola University.

Of course, by then I no longer had the edge to compete in the NBA; but that was okay. I was older and had a different perspective on life. What is amazing in all of this is how God preserved my eligibility (and enough of my game) to play college basketball so that when I decided to return to school as a legitimate student, my tuition would be covered. God did this, not so I would be chosen in the first round of the NBA draft, but so that I would be trained for *ministry* at one of the nation's top Christian universities. I now know that ministry was God's true design for my life all along.

Choosing the Right Course

Sadly we are often unable to embrace God's plan and design for our lives because we tend to focus on scoring points in the wrong game. It is so easy to become preoccupied with achieving personal success or pursuing selfish goals and dreams that we fail to consider the question: What does God want for my life?

Of course I am a firm believer in setting personal goals and working diligently to achieve those goals, but I am afraid that, far too often in our pursuit of success, we neglect to evaluate whether or not our goals are consistent with God's plan. From a biblical perspective, the priority in life is not to excel in the stadium of selfish ambition, but it is to win in the arena of God's will. It is impossible to choose God's will when we view life through the lens of our own goals and aspirations. As long as our perspective is rooted in the transitory values of this world and not the eternal values of heaven, God's purposes for our lives will remain hidden.

In the quest for personal transformation, we cannot overlook the power of perspective. Perspective determines priorities, which in turn dictates choices. The way in which we see things is the source of the way in which we determine what is important. Of course what we deem important becomes the basis for determining our life choices.

As a kid, my perspective was simple: success in basketball meant success in life. As a result of this perspective, I valued whatever I thought would help me achieve my personal goals. The choices that I made reflected what I valued; and for many years I made selfish decisions that were designed to propel me closer to the NBA, but not closer to God.

Now suppose you decide to take a hiking trip from San Antonio, Texas, to Fargo, North Dakota. Imagine that on this trip you have no road map or tour guide. In fact, the only thing you have to provide direction is a compass. With determination and resolve you set out to reach your destination. As you make your way north, you soon realize that the compass is your most valuable possession. You trust this instrument with your life. You depend solely on it to point you in the right direction.

But suppose there is a slight defect with the magnetic needle. Instead of pointing north, without you realizing it, your compass guides you slightly northeast. While you think you are moving closer to Fargo, in reality you are traveling further and further off course!

You may be determined to reach your destination. But determination will not get you to North Dakota. You may even make progress each day. But what good is progress if you are moving in the wrong direction? You see, the problem is not with your desire or determination to reach your destination. The problem is that a defective compass is influencing you—and leading you off course.

In one sense, perspective is like an internal compass. It influences your will. And whether you realize it or not, that which influences your will the most determines the direction of your life. You may have a desire and determination to be different, but if your internal compass is defective, you will continue to make choices that lead in the wrong direction.

When we view life through the lens of eternity, we tend to make choices that are in line with God's purposes and that are on course with his divine destination for our lives. On the other hand, when life is viewed solely through the lens of personal goals, experiences or expectations, even when we think we are progressing, in reality, we are moving further off the course that God has established for us.

As believers the navigational tool that ensures the accuracy of our internal compass is biblical truth. We must therefore learn to cultivate an eternal perspective by bringing our minds into consistent and meaningful contact with the Word of God. The apostle Paul drives this point home with conviction and clarity as he addresses a mixed group of Jewish and Gentile believers living in Rome during the first century A.D. In his letter addressed to the church at Rome, Paul writes:

> And do not be conformed to this world, but be transformed by the renewing of your mind, that you may prove what the will of God is, that which is good and acceptable and perfect. (Romans 12:2)

Talk about perspective! This verse lays it out. Let's take a closer look at this passage.

A CULTURE OF MORAL DECAY

At the time this letter was written, not only were the institutionalized values and socially acceptable modes of thought of Roman culture corrupt and decadent, but they were rapidly infiltrating the Christian community. In an effort to warn Christians against being absorbed into this climate of moral decay, Paul calls for a change of perspective.

This new way of viewing things would be the key to freedom from a life of mediocrity and conformity. It would also serve as the internal compass that pointed Christians to the center of God's will. Paul's admonition to the church at Rome challenged them to make several crucial choices.

RESISTING THE PRESSURE TO CONFORM

First, Paul challenges them to resist the pressure from the world to be conformed to its image by admonishing them in the first part of Romans 12:2, "And be not conformed to this world." The word *conform* used in this verse is a very interesting Greek verb. It literally means to be squeezed, shaped or fashioned to fit the mold or image of something. Picture for a moment a skilled sculptor hard at work on a piece of clay. As the sculptor applies pressure through relentless pounding, squeezing and shaping, the clay begins to take on the shape that the sculptor has in mind.

If the sculptor wants the clay to become a figure of a man or woman, or an elephant for that matter, he simply squeezes and fashions the clay into that particular shape. It may take a while, but eventually his goal is accomplished. The sculptor controls what the clay becomes.

In the same way that a sculptor controls what a piece of clay becomes, the world's master sculptor, the devil, is hard at work on Christians, squeezing, pounding and applying pressure in an effort to control what we become. Paul says we are to resist this pressure.

Some time ago, I bought a container of Play-Doh molding clay for my kids. One night during our family time, we decided to try it out. It was great! We were all amazed at each other's ability to mold and fashion that clump of clay into various shapes and objects. What I discovered, however, was that the softer the clay, the easier it was to manipulate into the shapes we wanted.

When Paul says "be not conformed to this world," he is shouting, "Stop!" "Stop becoming a soft piece of clay in the hands of the enemy!" He is commanding us to stop allowing the devil to determine our perspective, to stop our drift toward what we were never designed to be—worldly.

WORLDLINESS

Worldliness among Christians is not a new phenomenon. In every generation, worldliness has been a problem. This was the case in Paul's day, and it is true today. One of the most effective methods that the enemy uses to defeat us and neutralize our witness for Christ is to lure us into a mindset that agrees with principles and values that represent his kingdom as opposed to God's.

Dr. Clinton E. Arnold, professor of New Testament at Talbot School of Theology, writes:

> Struggle with the evil one is a characteristic part of the life of every Christian in his or her effort to please and obey the Lord. Even after we are redeemed by the power and grace of the Lord Jesus Christ, Satan does not give up on us. His goal is to re-enslave us into a life of sinful disobedience against God, thus nullifying the level of impact we can have on the world for the cause of Christ.[1]

One way Satan is able to accomplish this is by bombarding us with messages and images that subtly or blatantly contradict biblical truths and values. This frontal assault by the enemy creates an erosion of our convictions and conditions us to be more susceptible to and tolerant of the world's philosophy of doing things.

Satan then uses the steady stream of information that flows through the media, music, literature, entertainment, sports, fashion, our educational system and politics for one underlying purpose: to control our point of view! Once Satan gains control of the grid through which we process the information of life, he is able to dictate the way in which we interpret and respond to that information.

We are warned in Scripture to be on the alert against the devil because, like a roaring lion, he roams the earth seeking someone to devour (1 Peter 5:8). The Bible also admonishes us to put on the full armor of God in order to protect ourselves from being manipulated by the "wiles" or mental tricks that Satan uses to promote his agenda through our lives (Ephesians 6:11). When we are more influenced by the world than we are by the Word of God, it is only a matter of time before we are squeezed and shaped into something other than what God designed us to be.

IT'S DEEPER THAN WE THINK

As Christians, we often have a superficial understanding of what worldliness is all about. As such, it is common for us to compile mental lists of "do's" and "don'ts" in an effort to gauge ourselves (and others) to determine if we are tipping the balance on the scale of worldliness. But worldliness cannot be relegated to an arbitrary list of activities. Worldliness is not just about having a pierced ear or tattoo-decorated body. Nor is listening to hip-hop music or dressing in the latest FUBU fashion attire synonymous with worldliness. Common activities, such as dancing or even drinking an occasional glass of wine do not capture the essence of worldliness. While these things may indicate the presence of worldliness, the issue of worldliness is far deeper.

Worldliness has to do with our spiritual allegiance. As Christians we belong to the kingdom of God. Therefore we must never defect to the other side. To do so is to once again pledge our allegiance to the demonic flag of hell under which we rallied before we trusted Christ as Lord. Instead we are to be faithful soldiers of the cross. We are to be living expressions of God's transforming power—through a life of obedience and submission to God's will. When we misplace our allegiance (by turning to the world), we are actively committing spiritual treason against God and his kingdom.

When it comes to worldliness, the issue has never been what we do; it has always been why we do it. It is not about what we wear; it is why we wear it. The problem is not necessarily the music we listen to (although sometimes this can be a problem in and of itself), but the issue is why we are listening in the first place.

Worldliness has always been about allegiance. To whom or what we commit our loyalty, devotion and fidelity is what's at stake. The world system, which is run by Satan, is not satisfied with merely manipulating the moral climate and social agenda of the culture. The ultimate goal is to sabotage the redemptive purposes of God through distracting, diverting and destroying God's people.

The apostle Paul is saying to the Christians at Rome and to us today, "Do not abandon the post!" He is saying, "Do not forfeit the impact and influence that your life was meant to have for the kingdom because of the affection and allegiance that you have for this world." Worldly Christians are a dime a dozen. But rare is the man or woman whose heartbeat throbs with the pulse of eternity. Scarce is the one who is driven not by the shifting tides of this present age but whose anchor is buried deep on the shores of heaven. When we allow the world to determine our perspective, we become prime candidates for disillusionment, disappointment and defeat.

RENEWING OUR MINDS

Second, Paul challenges the Christians in Rome to reprogram their thinking. He writes in the second part of Romans 12:2, "But be transformed by the renewing of your mind." The struggle to change worldly habits, attitudes and behaviors has plagued Christians for ages. Just as the Christians in Rome faced the dilemma of being absorbed into the moral decadence of their culture, the pressure to dance to the tune of this evil generation is a constant threat to us today.

In my own life I am shocked at the number of times I catch myself thinking in a manner not consistent with the biblical convictions that I hold dear. It may happen while I am watching a movie, listening to music or even during Sunday morning worship! Whatever the case, I realize that if I am not careful I could very easily allow the influence of the world to determine my perspective.

The solution to this pressure to conform, according to the apostle Paul, is to experience a radical transformation in our lives. The word *transformed* in this verse is the Greek word *metamorphoses*, which means to experience a radical, drastic change at the most basic and fundamental level of our beings. Just as a caterpillar is transformed from a fuzzy little worm into a beautiful butterfly, we are commanded to allow God's Spirit to perform spiritual surgery on our minds to change the way we think and thus transform our character and behavior into the holy character of Christ.

The imperative in Romans 12:2 is to change. The process, however, involves a qualitative renovation of how we think: the renewing of the mind. (I will discuss this in greater detail in chapter six.) What I find fascinating is that the imperative or command to change is written in the passive voice. The passive voice in Greek represents the subject as receiving the action of the verb. Based on this grammatical construction, personal transformation is not something that we do; rather it is something that we experience. The primary effort is not in forcing ourselves to change; rather it is giving God, through the person of the Holy Spirit, something to work with!

In the final analysis we are incapable of changing ourselves by ourselves. It is God through his Word and his Spirit who empowers us to accomplish the task. Our job is to cooperate with God by getting into his Word. When we read, study and apply God's Word to our lives, the Spirit of God has the ammunition he needs to renovate the grid through which we process life. Before long our perspective begins to change, our priorities shift and our choices start to reflect God's agenda and not our own. This is transformation.

Back in the day when I was chasing "hoop dreams," what I needed more than anything was a change of perspective. Fortunately that is precisely what happened. On a hot, muggy night in 1976, I trusted Jesus Christ as my Lord and Savior. As I began to read and apply God's Word to my life, God began performing spiritual surgery on my mind. Slowly I started seeing things differently.

I began to see that the universe did not revolve around my ambitions. I realized that even if I became the Michael Jordan of my generation, apart from Christ I would be empty and hollow inside. Once my perspective began to change, my priorities shifted, and when my priorities shifted, I discovered a new value system upon which to base my choices in life.

STAYING FOCUSED

It is impossible to absorb the constant barrage of worldly messages and not be affected in some way. Apart from a healthy dosage of God's Word to sanitize our thinking, our perspective will become clouded by the world.

A few years ago I was having trouble driving at night. At first I dismissed the whole thing as coincidence and attributed it to fatigue or poor lighting. But after a couple of missed exits on the freeway and a near collision on a busy street, I decided to have my eyes checked. The results of the eye examination confirmed my suspicions. I needed to wear prescription glasses. Without realizing it, my vision had become slightly out of focus. My new glasses solved the problem. Once I put the glasses on, to my amazement, I was able to clearly see things that had become blurred.

What those prescription glasses did for my eyes, the Word of God does for my perspective! We live in a culture that exerts tremendous pressure on Christians to conform to its values and standards. Occasionally we all tend to lose sight of God's objectives for our lives. There are times when the will of God becomes dim and blurry to us. When that happens we need God's Word to bring things back into focus.

When we read, study and apply God's Word under the guiding influence of the Spirit of God, it is like putting on a pair of spiritual glasses. The Spirit of God shows us, through the Word of God, who we are and what we are to be about in this world. The Word of God brings reality back into focus.

CONFIRMING THE WILL OF GOD

Finally, the apostle Paul challenges the Christians in Rome to confirm the will of God through living a transformed life. He writes at the end of Romans 12:2, "That you may prove what the will of God is, that which is good and acceptable and perfect." The whole point of experiencing a personal transformation is to glorify God and to allow him to accomplish his will through our lives.

It is frightening to think that we could easily slip through the cracks of life without ever accomplishing the will of God. This is particularly true in America where the definition of success is often understood in the context of material abundance and prosperity. We live in a culture that is driven with passion to acquire wealth, status and power. But I ask you: is being successful according to the standards of the world all there is to life? I don't think so!

God did not put us here that we might become preoccupied with personal pursuits. The goal of life is not to achieve personal success. The goal is not to get rich. The goal in life is to bring our wills into alignment with the will of God that we might become instruments through which God accomplishes his goals and achieves his purposes.

If you thought that God created you solely for the purpose of gratifying selfish and inappropriate goals and objectives, you missed the point. We are not here to impress others with our success but to accomplish the will of God through a transformed life of faithful service.

What is your perspective in life? Are you peering at life through the lens of the temporal? Or do you see through the eyes of eternity? If the former is true, that may explain why you are unable to experience lasting peace, joy, contentment or transformation. If the latter is the case, I encourage you: stay the course.

This world is not our home. We are not permanent citizens of earth. We are citizens of heaven. Never should we think and live as though we are bound to the temporal. Instead our perspective, our priorities and our choices must be shaped by eternal values. When we maintain an eternal perspective, ultimately the choices that we make will guide us into the center of God's will. And it is in the center of the will of God that we find joy, peace and purpose.

5 || Consider It All Joy

It began as a normal morning for Rick and Judy Taylor. Rick was director of Christian camping at Pine Cove Christian Conference Center near Tyler, Texas, where they lived. Judy and their three young sons—Kyle (age five-and-a-half), Bryan (three-and-a-half) and Eric (two-and-a-half)—had just finished breakfast at the center. The boys asked if they could get their tricycles, which were parked about one hundred feet from their home. "Okay," Judy replied, "but come right back."

Judy was the type of mom who never let her kids out of her sight. But she was feeling fatigued from her late-term pregnancy, and she had to rewrap a birthday present one of the boys had mistakenly unwrapped the night before.

A few minutes passed, and suddenly she felt something was wrong. She honked the horn of the family van and called the boys. Then she noticed Bryan walking through the woods crying. "Bryan, what's wrong? Where are your brothers?"

"They're dying in the water."

When Rick and Judy later pieced the story together, they

learned that the boys had wandered down to a pond on the property, a deep spill-off from a dam that was filled with cold, murky water. Eric had tripped and rolled down a steep bank into the water, and Kyle had jumped in to save him, yelling for Bryan to go get help.

By the time Judy reached the pond, the water was deceptively calm. She waded in, trying to find someone, but got stuck in the mud. Bryan was screaming, thinking something would happen to her too, but she grabbed some plants to pull herself out.

Feeling totally helpless, Judy looked up to heaven and yelled, "Please don't take two!" Immediately Eric's body broke the surface of the water, and she dove in despite her pregnancy to pull him out. His body was totally limp and blue; he wasn't breathing, and his heart wasn't beating.

Frantically she performed CPR on Eric. After a few minutes, she picked him up in frustration, held him over her left arm and hit his back. At that point he began gasping and coughing, then immediately went into shock.

Judy thought she had just witnessed a miracle. But now she was faced with the most terrible choice of her life: Kyle had still not surfaced, and she needed to rush Eric to the hospital if he was to live.

"This is what I have to do," she told Bryan. "We have to say goodbye to Kyle right now." And so to save one son, she was forced to leave another in the pond. She carried Eric to the van and then tore through the grounds looking for Rick. He had just left a meeting when he looked up and saw the van barreling toward him. *Something is wrong,* he thought.

The van slid to a stop on the gravel of the parking lot, and Rick heard Judy cry out the words that changed his life: "Kyle is dead, and Eric is dying!"

They rushed Eric to the hospital, where doctors worked frantically on him for twenty-four hours before they determined he would live. Doctors estimated he was underwater for at least fifteen minutes. Fortunately some trapped air in his stomach allowed oxygen to continue reaching his brain, and that was also what brought him back to the surface.

In the meantime searchers found Kyle's body, and the Taylors were left to grieve the loss of their firstborn son.[1]

What happened that day changed the lives of Rick and Judy Taylor forever. What happened that day also serves as a sober reminder to all of us that life is unpredictable, and the winds of adversity do not discriminate as they sweep across the landscape of human experience.

Potentially, devastation is but one moment away from each of us. When devastation strikes, what distinguishes those of us who have a relationship with God from those who do not is perspective. Even under adversity, we have the ability to factor God and his purposes, plan, timing and objectives into the equation of life.

God is the sovereign ruler of the universe. Not only does God control what happens in the world, he also controls what happens in our individual lives. With God there are no mistakes, mishaps or random acts of chance. When bad things happen to us, we must recognize that God has a plan and a purpose for allowing it.

Internalizing this truth gives us a deeper appreciation for the fact that nothing can enter into our lives without first being filtered through the grid of God's perfect or permissive will for us. Such an understanding drastically alters how we view our circumstances. No longer do we see tragedy, difficulties and problems as debilitating obstacles but as divine opportunities to experience God.

This is an important lesson for us to grasp. How we view our problems, by and large, determines our response to them. This principle is taught in the book of James. In the first few verses of James 1, we are instructed to view our problems not through the eyes of despair, but through the lens of delight. James says, "Consider it all joy, my brethren, when you encounter various trials, knowing that the testing of your faith produces endurance" (James 1:2-3). According to James, there are three realities concerning difficult circumstances that cannot be ignored.

THE CERTAINTY OF DIFFICULTIES

First, there is the certainty of difficulties. James does not say, "Consider it all joy my brethren, *if* you encounter various trials" but *"when* you encounter various trials." The truth of the matter is that if we live long enough we will encounter circumstances that cause deep hurt, profound disappointment and excruciating pain. This is an indisputable and unavoidable reality, even among Christians. It may contradict some folks' theology, but let's be honest, bad things do happen to good people.

I have learned through the years that much of what happens in my own life falls outside my sphere of influence. No matter how cautious, careful, deliberate, alert or calculating I may be, there are times when things happen that are simply beyond my ability to explain or control. This is the nature of life. We will have difficulties.

THE DIVERSITY OF DIFFICULTIES

Second, we see the diversity of difficulties. The word *various* is a Greek word meaning multicolored; the idea is that problems hit us from all angles with different shades of intensity. In other words the impact and occurrence of difficulties is not restricted to one area of our lives; instead our problems are diverse, affecting our families, finances, careers, health, ministries—the list is endless.

Most of us have never had to deal with the painful circumstances of losing a child, as was the case with Rick and Judy Taylor. Yet disappointment, hurt and a sense of loss can touch us in a variety of ways.

Meet Rasheed and Tonya Barnes. Rasheed is a former athlete who loves sports. He still plays an occasional pick up game of basketball or soccer, but mainly Rasheed channel surfs, hoping to catch all of his favorite teams on the tube. Rasheed professes to be a believer, but he will admit that he has no interest in reading the Bible or attending church. For Rasheed, spiritual things are not that important.

Tonya, on the other hand, is the product of a strong Christian home. She is committed to her little community church where she sings in the choir and teaches young adult Sunday school. Tonya regularly reads her Bible and rarely misses a service on Sunday morning. For Tonya, the most important aspect of life is her walk with the Lord.

Jason, the couple's seven-year-old son, is beginning to show interest in spiritual things. Tonya feels it's important for Jason to come to church with her so that he can learn more about the Bible. It is Rasheed's opinion that what Jason needs is a dose of male bonding. He insists that Jason hang out with him at home. The couple argues constantly over this, as well as other issues, and neither person is willing to compromise.

Several months pass without any resolution to their problems. Now, both Rasheed and Tonya are tense and under a lot of pressure in the relationship. It seems that even the smallest disagreement escalates into a nasty argument. In their ten years of marriage, Tonya cannot recall things ever being this bad between them.

Finally, one night after putting Jason to bed, Tonya decides it's time to talk about their problems. She is nervous and unsure about how Rasheed will respond. After taking several deep breaths and whispering a prayer, she musters up enough courage to approach Rasheed.

Rasheed is on the sofa. He has a blank stare on his face. The lighting in the room is dim, and there is a strange stillness hovering in the air. Tonya enters the room. But Rasheed barely acknowledges her presence. After several long moments it is Rasheed who breaks the silence. "Tonya," his voice is cold and indifferent, "I want a divorce. I will pack my things in the morning and move out by the end of the week." He gets up and walks away, leaving his wife sitting in the dark speechless, confused and alone.

Whether it is the death of a loved one or the death of a marriage, the reality of life demands that we encounter a diversity of problems that have the potential to crush us spiritually, emotionally, physically and psychologically. The question is not if these circumstances will come. The question is how we will respond to such circumstances when they come.

THE PRODUCTIVITY OF PROBLEMS

This leads to the third reality concerning difficult circumstances: the productivity associated with difficulties. Notice again what James says, "Knowing that the testing of your faith produces endurance" (James 1:3). This may seem strange, but there is inherent value in difficulties and trials. God, in his sovereignty, chooses to use the pressures, problems and pain of life as crucibles to produce depth of character in us. In the same way that extreme heat rids a precious metal such as gold of its impurities, the fires of testing burn away the dross in our lives, refining our character so that God is able to use us as tools to impact others for the kingdom.

Character is what gives us credibility in the sight of God and humanity. And it is difficult circumstances that produce this valuable commodity in our lives. It wasn't easy for Rick and Judy Taylor to embrace the crushing circumstance that robbed them of their firstborn. But out of that tragedy, God forged a depth of character and faith that allows Rick and Judy to be used as instruments of hope in the lives of others.

Today, the catastrophic event that changed Rick's and Judy's lives has become a powerful source of encouragement for many as the Taylors share their story with thousands at conferences across the country.[2] How were the Taylors able to turn a tragedy into a triumph? It all boils down to one thing: perspective.

Rasheed Barnes decided to walk away from his marriage. But what about Tonya? Will she walk away from her painful circumstances bitter, emotionally crippled and wounded for life? Or will she cling to God, trusting him to journey with her through a most difficult period? Again the answer hinges primarily on one thing: perspective.

A proper perspective gives us a willingness and resolve to bear the difficulties of life with a hopeful, expectant attitude. With the right perspective, we are able to move forward in life despite our problems. In fact the word *patience* used in James 1:3 can be translated as *endurance* or *perseverance*. It is a Greek word that literally means "to abide under." This word refers to an internal quality that does not surrender to circumstances.

When James says, "Consider it all joy, my brethren, when you encounter various trials, knowing that the testing of your faith produces endurance," he is screaming, "Get perspective!" He is shouting, "View difficulties with joy—literally gladness of heart!" As we go through painful situations, we are able to hang tough, but not because we possess some strength or power of our own. We are able to withstand the weight and pressure of trying circumstances because we understand that adversity is an up-close and personal opportunity to experience the power, presence and purpose of God—as he faithfully produces character in our lives.

Facing problems and difficulties is a part of life. Perspective is what keeps us from succumbing to our circumstances when we feel overwhelmed. When we see our difficulties, problems and challenges as opportunities to sulk, complain or become angry, we soon slip into a dark pit of despair. But when we view our problems as opportunities to experience God, we climb to higher heights of personal growth, maturity and productivity.

Nelson Mandela, the great human rights activist and champion for racial justice, faced some difficult challenges in his life. In 1964 Mandela was convicted of sedition and sentenced to life in prison. Without hope for parole, Mandela was sent to Robben Island, a harsh penal colony across from Cape Town's harbor in South Africa.

During the first ten years of his imprisonment, Nelson Mandela swung a pickax in a limestone quarry breaking boulders into gravel. Yet he never lost sight of his mission. Even under the brutal conditions of prison, Mandela's commitment to racial justice never flagged.

Unlike many of us who would have succumbed to the limitations of our environments, given up hope or felt justified in nursing a spirit of bitterness, Mandela instead became a crusader for better prison conditions. What is more, for nearly three decades Nelson Mandela led the struggle to topple South Africa's apartheid regime from behind prison bars.[3]

What made the difference in this man's life? How was he able to persevere despite adverse conditions? Again the answer is perspective. Nelson Mandela saw himself in light of his mission as opposed to his misfortune! As a result he did not allow his circumstances or conditions to determine his level of productivity or the destiny of his life.

Nelson Mandela, Rick and Judy Taylor, and countless others are living proof that, in this life, it's not so much what happens to us that's important, but it's how we respond to what happens that matters most. And just as Nelson Mandela and the Taylors overcame incredible odds to accomplish their life missions, we too can rise above difficult circumstances, challenges and limitations to accomplish the goals that God has for our lives. Perspective is the key!

6 || Let the Walls Come Down!

D avid has struggled for years with anger. Whenever he is in a threatening situation or someone disagrees with his point of view, hostility wells up inside. At times David becomes so angry that his body shakes.

David's many attempts to change his destructive behavior have resulted only in frustration. It seems that no matter how hard David tries to gain control over his anger, he continues to live on the edge—one breath away from an emotional explosion. David is in bondage. He is aware of the need to change, but he feels totally helpless to do anything about his problem. What is the reason for David's failure? He is wrestling with what is known as a stronghold in his mind.

STRONGHOLDS

Most of us are familiar with the term *stronghold,* but I wonder if we fully understand the tremendous influence that a stronghold exerts upon us, particularly when it comes to making choices that result in personal transformation. David, for example, is aware that his anger is out of control and is constantly getting him into trouble. But David's awareness of his problem and desire to change is not sufficient to alter his behavior.

The fact is that David's choices are being influenced by a negative pattern of thought and response that is burned in his mind. It is this deeply rooted negative thought process, or stronghold, that is causing David to repeat behavior that he hates, despite his desires or desperate attempts to change.

What exactly is a stronghold? The word itself is an ancient military term depicting a fortified city where residents were able to find refuge and safety during times of war. In those days, it was strategic to build a city on a hill with an impenetrable wall of stone surrounding it. The objective of the location and fortification was to barricade the city, protecting its citizens, treasure and resources against invading armies.

Defenders within the fortified city could successfully foil an outside military threat due to the opposing army's inability to penetrate the wall. As long as the invasion was limited to a perimeter outside the wall, the base of operations inside was uninterrupted, and the city remained safe and intact. A fortified city became known as a stronghold.

In spiritual warfare, Satan has established a "city" in our minds. There he sets up his base of operations against us. This city is surrounded and fortified by a formidable, impenetrable ideological fortress of ideas, speculations and reasonings erected by Satan to guard and protect the most valuable resource that he uses to keep us in bondage: our thoughts.

Satan's objective is to keep the invading, liberating truth of God's Word from penetrating beyond his diabolical wall of influence in our minds. When Satan is successful, his city remains intact. His base of operation is uninterrupted, and the negative process of thought and response that he uses to keep us in bondage continues to exert a powerful influence upon our wills.

BURNED INTO OUR MINDS

Dr. Neil T. Anderson describes a stronghold as a negative pattern of thought which is burned into our minds either through repetition or through one-time traumatic experiences. "Once a stronghold of thought and response is entrenched in your mind," says Dr. Anderson, "your ability to choose and to act contrary to that pattern is virtually non-existent."[1] This explains why there are many people, like David, who remain in bondage to negative behavior, even though they have a genuine desire to be different.

In order for positive change to occur in our lives, we must learn to exert our will through the power of positive choice. But what makes a stronghold so devastating and disruptive is that its influence overrides our desires, good intentions and efforts to accomplish this goal. In fact the powerful influence of a stronghold renders our resolve and strength of will impotent to make choices that result in growth and transformation.

This is because, when a negative thought pattern is firmly established in the mind, once the pattern is triggered the process that leads to failure becomes automatic. It is like hitting the switch that activates the autopilot mechanism of an airplane. Once the switch is turned on, the plane basically flies itself.

In a similar sense, when we are locked in the trap of a spiritual stronghold, once the negative thought pattern is triggered our actions go into the autopilot mode. Subconsciously we relinquish control of our voluntary will, and we are then driven along by an involuntary process that predetermines our choices and responses.

Whenever David's anger erupts, it is because at some point in his mind the auto-response switch was flipped. Each time this switch is triggered, a series of responses automatically kicks in, piloting David's choices to a familiar destination—destructive behavior. David feels like a helpless passenger enduring a turbulent ride that invariably ends with disaster.

Perhaps you feel like an involuntary passenger on a bumpy ride of your own. Your issue may not be anger or hostility, but a stronghold can produce a variety of negative behaviors that are just as disastrous. For instance, do you worry a lot? If so, then you must realize that anxiety is a stronghold that demonstrates a lack of faith and reveals a problem you have with control.

Another common stronghold is depression. Depression, when it is not produced by a chemical imbalance, is basically an expression of hopelessness.[2] Certain trigger points set off the thought and response process which lead to destructive behavior. For example, Brandon and Teresa Jordan have been married five years. For the past year Brandon has slipped into depression whenever a certain love song came on the radio. It turns out that early in the marriage Teresa admitted to having an affair. Brandon was devastated by his wife's confession and felt hopelessly rejected. The night Teresa told of the affair, the love song was playing in the background. Now, whenever Brandon hears that song it triggers traumatic memories leading to bouts with depression.

THE ROOT CAUSES OF STRONGHOLDS

Again, a stronghold can be the result of long-term exposure to the environment, or it can be the result of a brief but traumatic experience. In Brandon's case, his depression is the result of a traumatic experience that is triggered by a certain song. But how did David get locked into his struggle with anger?

I found out that David was raised in a hostile environment.

David's father was angry and disappointed with life. What's more, David's father took his frustration out on his family. Often he would yell and scream at his son for no reason. As David grew older, the abuse grew worse and resulted in nasty arguments. The verbal assaults by his father left David feeling wounded and rejected. Eventually deep-seated anger replaced the hurt that David felt.

As a kid, David learned to respond to conflict by lashing out. Now, as an adult, those thought and response patterns, which were developed over a long period of time have become strongholds that are deeply entrenched in his mind.

We are all susceptible to strongholds in the mind. It may be a stronghold of anger or depression. Or it could be a host of other fortresses, such as racism, an inferiority complex, laziness, sexual promiscuity, an unforgiving spirit, hostility, homosexuality, anorexia, greed and materialism, pride, gluttony, drug addiction and so on. The list is endless. The results are the same: a deep sense of hopelessness stemming from the inability to break the power of a bad habit or negative behavior that is ruining our lives.

SATAN'S STRATEGY

Satan knows the power and effectiveness of a stronghold. That is why he stands at the threshold of our minds, poised and eager to unleash a barrage of seductive ideas and suggestions into our thoughts. This satanic assault on the mind is designed to influence our wills.

According to Dr. Neil Anderson, Satan has a two-prong strategy that he uses to erect strongholds in our minds. First, Satan aggressively attempts to introduce his thoughts and ideas into our minds. Once successful, he works to deceive us into believing that his thoughts are our own or even God's. Second, Satan vigorously reinforces and fortifies those negative patterns of thought that we have already established in our minds as a result of living a life independent of God.[3]

You see, when you became a child of God, you went from being a sinner to a saint. Now that does not mean you became a perfect person who no longer sins. It does mean, however, that you were saved by grace and set apart for the purposes of God. In the moment that you trusted Christ as Lord and Savior, you entered into a whole new reality.

But before you became a child of God or a saint, you were simply a sinner—naturally influenced by the world, the flesh and the devil. With each passing day you became more and more conditioned to think and behave a certain way. How you processed information and responded to life was self-serving and independent of God.

Now, even though you are a Christian and you have a new nature, your predisposition to think and act independent of God (based on how you were conditioned by the world), remains deeply embedded in your mind.[4]

TEARING DOWN STRONGHOLDS

Overcoming strongholds in the mind is a difficult task, and in some cases it may take years to accomplish. The good news is that God has not abandoned us to fight this battle on our own. Indeed, God has put at our disposal divinely powerful weapons specifically designed to destroy the strongholds that lock us into negative patterns of thinking and behaving.

Of course these are not your ordinary weapons of war. But we are not engaged in an ordinary battle. The battle for the mind is a spiritual battle. We must therefore be equipped with an arsenal of spiritual weapons. That is precisely what God has provided for us!

The apostle Paul acknowledges this.

For though we walk in the flesh, we do not war according to the flesh, for the weapons of our warfare are not of the flesh, but divinely powerful for the destruction of fortresses. We are destroying speculations and every lofty thing raised up against the knowledge of God, and we are taking every thought captive to the obedience of Christ. (2 Corinthians 10:3-5)

According to the Bible, we can destroy the strongholds in our minds. Yes, we can pull down those speculations and reasonings that keep us in bondage! All we need to do is pick up the weapons that God has provided. What are these divinely powerful weapons? They are the power of truth (which is the Word of God), the power of prayer and the power of the Holy Spirit. It's time to take a look at how these weapons work.

7 || It's All in the Mind

Carla is almost forty. She is a wife and mother of three. On the surface Carla appears to have it all together; she has a loving husband, a wonderful family and a charming personality. To her friends, Carla seems so happy. The truth is that Carla's life is a wreck.

For years Carla has struggled with depression and low self-esteem. At times she is so overwhelmed by the normal pressures of life that she does not bother to get out of bed. Carla has a dark secret that she has kept for years. At age ten, Carla's stepfather began molesting her. He did not stop until she went away to college.

Carla never told anyone about her stepfather. Now, as an adult, no matter how hard she tries to get on with her life, these painful memories of the past keep her paralyzed. Like an evil stalker lurking in the hidden shadows of her mind, the traumatic thoughts of betrayal and feelings of guilt mock her every move. Carla feels like a prisoner; she is chained to a world of regret.

Unfortunately Carla is not alone in her prison. Just look

around you. Untold numbers of people remain stuck in a world of pain and disappointment. Many never recover from their scars. Others manage to limp through life maimed by the crippling disease of apathy, cynicism and indifference. Still others, like Carla, spend years incarcerated inside the restricted walls of self-imposed limitations, bad habits, self-destructive behaviors and negative attitudes.

Do you know someone like Carla? Someone who is caught in a moment of pain that refuses to let him or her go? Perhaps you have a peculiar limp of your own. If so, I strongly urge you to keep reading. The next couple of chapters are tailor-made for you. In the pages that follow, we will attempt to identify strongholds and uproot the stakes of bondage so deeply buried in the folds of our minds. For ultimately, the battle for change is a struggle that's taking place in the mind.

WE BECOME WHAT WE THINK

During the 1960s the Green Bay Packers, under the tutelage of legendary coach Vince Lombardi, dominated the National Football League. The Packers, who were known for their toughness, discipline and ability to rise above adversity, earned the right to play in the first two Super Bowl games ever played. In each Super Bowl contest, the opposing teams pushed themselves to the limit in an effort to establish supremacy. In the end, the Packers walked away with the championship trophy.

The interesting thing is that the Green Bay Packers were not always a great team. In fact, at one point, they were considered the "chumps" of the league—losers, willing to settle for mediocrity—that is, until Coach Lombardi challenged their thinking. Once Lombardi got his team to the level of thinking like champions, a radical transformation occurred. Soon they began playing like champions![1]

Now understand that the Packers did not go from chumps to champions because they suddenly became better players. Coach Lombardi did not inject his team with an extra dose of talent or ability; they already possessed those qualities. What made these men different was a new way of thinking! The team experienced astounding results when they exchanged a negative belief system, conditioned by failure, for a positive belief system pregnant with expectation and possibility.

In the final analysis, whether in a football stadium or in the arena of life, we cannot subscribe to a defeated mindset and expect to experience a life of victory. Victorious living demands victorious thinking! A major reason why we live defeated lives is because we lock ourselves into defeated thinking.

As long as the Packers thought like losers, their performance suffered, and they actually played like losers. It wasn't until their thinking changed that their performance improved and the team began to excel. The truth is that people from all walks of life and various professional, social, economic and educational levels struggle in life because they subscribe to a defeated mindset.

Often a defeated mindset is the result of negative messages that have been singed in our memory banks from early childhood. As children, the words that our parents, teachers, coaches, classmates or siblings used to describe us can have a devastating impact on how we view ourselves. Harsh words such as "You're stupid!" "You're ugly!" "You're fat!" "You're lazy!" or "You will never amount to anything!" are powerful and can potentially set the stage for a life of pain and dysfunction.

It is common for us to carry emotional wounds and psychological scars into adult life as a result of childhood "programming." This is one reason why psychologists, psychiatrists and psychotherapists are in such high demand. What these trained professionals are able to do is treat mental or emotional disorders by helping people identify negative experiences, events or thoughts that contribute to their insecurity, low self-esteem or that trigger dysfunctional behavior. The goal is to eventually reprogram the thought process altogether. Why is this important? Our thought process is important because the way we think determines who we become.

Of course I do not agree with all the secular or clinical methods being used today to help people sort through their problems. However I do believe that it is vital to understand the link that exists between our thoughts and the people we become as a result of those thoughts.

THOUGHTS DETERMINE CHARACTER

As Christians most of us are aware that character is a very valuable commodity in the kingdom of God. This is true because God is primarily concerned with our hearts, not our appearance (1 Samuel 16:7). It is God's desire that we develop godly character during our stay on earth. What we must understand, however, is that our character—good, bad or indifferent—is a direct product of our minds or how we think.

Solomon, the ancient king of Israel and the wisest man who ever lived (except Christ), understood the connection between our thoughts and our character long before the topic became popular or clinical. Under the inspiration of the Holy Spirit, Solomon makes some rather insightful observations. Listen carefully to his remarks; they pack a heavy dose of wisdom: "Do not eat the bread of a selfish man, or desire his delicacies; for as he thinks within himself, so he is. He says to you, 'Eat and drink!' but his heart is not with you" (Proverbs 23:6-7).

Some time ago I dropped in on a friend unannounced during the dinner hour. Upon entering the house, my mouth began to water and my stomach churned as I smelled the roast beef simmering in the oven. On the dining table I noticed a delectable spread of macaroni and cheese, corn bread, green beans, candied yams and my favorite dessert . . . peach cobbler.

My friend's wife said to me, "Stay for dinner." But the scowl on her face said: "Go away!" Guess who didn't stay for dinner? Although this woman pretended to be hospitable, in her heart she resented the fact that I showed up when I did. In spite of what she said, it was the language of her heart that came to the surface, telling me that I was not welcome!

It is impossible to suppress indefinitely the language of the heart. This is Solomon's lesson. What is in the heart (the nature and quality of our thoughts) invariably determines who we become (the nature and quality of our character). We may attempt to disguise this truth through hypocrisy or pretense. But in the end our true colors will shine forth. Please understand this point: that which most dominates our mind becomes that which most determines our character. As a person thinks in his heart, *so is he!*

BEHAVIOR EXPOSES CHARACTER

While it is our thoughts that determine our character, it is our behavior, on the other hand, that exposes our character. Once again, listen to the words of Solomon:

> He who hates disguises it with his lips, but he lays up deceit in his heart. When he speaks graciously, do not believe him, for there are seven abominations in his heart. Though his hatred covers itself with guile, his wickedness will be revealed before the assembly. (Proverbs 26:24-26)

What Solomon is saying is that by our actions our character is exposed. No matter how charming our personality or how flattering our conversation, if what's in our heart or mind is wicked, then eventually those wicked character traits will come out.

For example, a thief is someone who is sneaky and has deceptive character traits. As a pastor I occasionally have the responsibility of counseling people who suffer from this particular problem. In dealing with such a person, it has been my observation that at some point behavior that is manipulative and dishonest will be exhibited. A thief may be skilled and sophisticated at concealing his problem; but eventually he will slip, and his actions will reveal his true character.

Or a man who habitually cheats on his wife is someone who obviously doesn't understand the meaning of commitment. Such a man is immoral and lacks strength of character. He may attempt to hide or cover up his sexual indiscretions with other women, but eventually he will be busted. And his cheating heart will land him in big trouble.

In this universe there are certain irrefutable laws. This is true in both the physical world as well as the spiritual realm. In the physical world, if you jump off a ten-story building, the law of gravity demands that your flight pattern be one directional: down! Gravity is a physical reality that cannot be disputed.

In a similar sense there are spiritual realities that cannot be denied. One such reality is that behavior exposes character. It may not happen right away; in some cases it may not happen for many years. But ultimately God will use our own actions to bring about disclosure of what is in our hearts.

I know this sounds strange. Particularly to a generation that is not rooted and grounded in the objective truth of God's Word. But the fact remains that light reveals what is hidden in darkness. Sooner or later the depth and quality of our character, or the lack thereof, will come to light.

In the 1980s, television evangelist Jimmy Swaggart was well

known for his fiery sermons and high moral standards. When Jim Bakker (former host of *The PTL Club*) admitted to having an affair, Swaggart—in what appeared to be righteous indignation—swiftly and severely blasted Bakker for his moral failure. It wasn't until Swaggart himself was cited for soliciting prostitutes some months later that his own demons of lust surfaced, exposing the flaws in his personal character.[2]

Ultimately God's greatest concern is with the condition of the heart: our character. It is character that God is in the process of shaping and molding into the image of Christ. When we have flaws in our character, God will expose them. He does this not to embarrass us but to make us aware of our total dependence on him to produce holiness in our lives. We are accountable to God not only for our actions but also for the character that produces our actions.

At times my kids shade the truth to keep from being punished. My advice to them is this: "It is better to tell the truth and deal with me than it is to lie and have to deal with God." Of course kids are not the only ones who need to heed that advice. As adults we are also prone to lapses in our judgment and character. Recently I was in my office at home when the phone began ringing. Usually I am not the one who answers incoming calls, but this time was different.

As I picked up the receiver in my office, simultaneously my daughter Kimya, who is seventeen, picked up the other phone in the kitchen. Of course the call was for her. I did not say anything, so Kimya was not aware that I was listening in. The guy who called, in my opinion, was rude and disrespectful. He was calling to invite Kimya to a house party that weekend. Kimya sort of giggled and agreed to come.

When the conversation ended, I called Kimya into my office and told her that I was listening to her conversation. I let her know that I did not approve of the language that the young man used. I also told her that she would not be attending that party. I was expecting a battle. Instead she responded by saying, "I was not intending to go in the first place."

"Why?" I asked.

To which she replied, "Because I don't like to be around that crowd."

"Then, you should not have lied to the young man," I responded. I then gave her a minilecture on character and integrity. I concluded with the admonition, "Always say what you mean and mean what you say."

About an hour or so later, a friend of mine called and invited Donna and me to a gathering that same weekend. I had no desire or intentions of attending. Yet I told my friend that we would try our best to make it. After hanging up the phone, the words that I had spoken to Kimya just one hour previous smashed against my brain: "Always say what you mean and mean what you say!" I realized immediately that I had blown it. What's more, God used that incident to expose a weakness in my own character. I quickly confessed my hypocrisy to God and asked for forgiveness.

Do not be deceived: God is meticulously thorough when it comes to exposing the character of our hearts. No matter how we try to camouflage or cover up what is inside, eventually God will expose the truth.

TRANSFORMED THINKING

Both our behavior and character are products of our minds. Because this is true, it is imperative that we learn to elevate the quality of our thoughts in order to develop the character traits and behavior patterns that are pleasing to God. Raising the quality of our thoughts is achieved only as we saturate our minds with the Word of God. The apostle Paul gives us the prescription. He writes:

> Finally, brethren, whatever is true, whatever is honorable, whatever is right, whatever is pure, whatever is lovely, whatever is of good repute, if there is any excellence and if anything worthy of praise, let your mind dwell on these things. (Philippians 4:8)

Did you catch that phrase "let your mind dwell on these things"? That is an important concept. The word *dwell* in this passage comes from a Greek verb that means to inhabit as one's abode. It refers to a person's mental address or that which most occupies a person's thoughts. We are all familiar with the expression "Get your mind out of the gutter." To say this to someone is to suggest that such a person is preoccupied with vulgar and often repulsive thoughts. For example, a person may become preoccupied with inappropriate, lustful fantasies. It could be said that this person's mind lives in the gutter.

When Paul says, "Let your mind dwell on these things," he is saying that as Christians our minds should never live in the gutter of worldliness nor should our thoughts reside in the sewer of mediocrity. Instead our mental zip code should inhabit the high moral ground of truth, honor, praise, faith, righteousness, purity, virtue and excellence. This is where we should live in our minds as Christians. These are the kinds of thoughts that will produce transformation in our lives.

Why is what we think about so important? Because it is the quality of our thoughts that determine the quality of our lives. Of course, factors such as genetics, culture and environment play a part in determining our caliber of life; nevertheless any hope of changing years of bad habits, negative attitudes or destructive behavior patterns must begin by changing the way we

think. Or as the apostle Paul puts it, "Be transformed by the renewing of your mind" (Romans 12:2).

In order to change the way we think, we must spend consistent time in the Word of God. Yet mere exposure to God's Word
is not enough. We must take it a step further. Let me suggest
three things:

Memorize the Word of God. First, we must memorize the
Word of God. Scripture memorization has a way of keeping our
thoughts connected to the mind of God. I do not have to convince you of the tendency we all have to revisit the old, run-
down neighborhood of carnal thoughts or to dwell in those dark
places in our minds. This capacity to mentally backslide is typical and often spontaneous.

The problem is that our minds are never in neutral. When
our minds are exposed to a stream of information that serves
only to reinforce old negative attitudes, we tend not to make
choices that set us free from the bondage of mediocrity. Instead
we become locked in a thought process that promotes familiar
bad habits and perpetuates destructive behavior.

The more of God's Word we have in our minds, the greater
our ability to identify with his plan and purposes. When we tap
into God's mind through memorizing his Word, our spiritual-
consciousness level is raised and we tend to think and process
things on a higher plane. We develop a biblical mindset. We
adopt a biblical worldview. We become better equipped to challenge personal mediocrity and resist the influences of an evil,
ungodly culture. When God's Word is firmly rooted in our
hearts and minds, we can respond to the challenges of life in a
manner that honors him.

In addition, Scripture memorization serves as a deterrent to
sin. In Psalm 119:11 King David says, "Thy Word have I trea-
sured in my heart, that I may not sin against you." Do you wish

to stop a sinful habit or attitude? Then start burying the Word of God deep into the folds of your mind. An aggressive program of memorizing Scripture forces us to relocate our thoughts from the ghetto of depravity into the neighborhood of the holy.

Meditate on the Word of God. Next, we must meditate on the Word of God.

> How blessed is the man who does not walk in the counsel of the wicked,
> Nor stand in the path of sinners,
> Nor sit in the seat of the scoffers!
> But his delight is in the law of the LORD,
> And in His law he meditates day and night.
> And he will be like a tree *firmly* planted by streams of water,
> Which yields its fruit in its season,
> And its leaf does not wither;
> And in whatever he does, he prospers. (Psalm 1:1-3)

> This book of the law shall not depart from your mouth, but you shall meditate on it day and night, so that you may be careful to do according to all that is written in it; for then you will make your way prosperous, and then you will have success. (Joshua 1:8)

In these passages of Scripture we are taught that when we meditate on the Word of God, God promises to open the windows of heaven and lavish us with rich blessings. This does not mean that meditating on the Word of God is a quick fix to our problems or that it is an easy formula for success. To meditate on the Word of God involves work, commitment and a plan of implementation. It is not merely an accumulation of information.

The word *meditate* carries the idea of pondering, contemplating or considering. It is a word that denotes engaging the mind, not in a superficial or casual way but in a deep and meaningful way. To meditate on God's Word means to reflect seriously on what it is saying—to linger thoughtfully on its promises, its precepts and its principles, as well as its warnings and prohibitions.

To meditate on the Word of God, then, is to exchange our thoughts and perspectives for the mind of Christ. It is to weigh everything we say or do in light of what God says about the subject. When we do this, we cannot help but develop the mind of Christ; and when we have the mind of Christ, we cannot help but follow God's will. Of course when we choose God's will, we become prime candidates for God's blessings in God's timing!

Mimic the character of God. Finally, we must mimic God's character as it is revealed in his Word: "Therefore be imitators of God, as beloved children; and walk in love, just as Christ also loved you, and gave Himself up for us, an offering and a sacrifice to God as a fragrant aroma" (Ephesians 5:1-2). We mimic the character of God when we internalize his Word and begin imitating the pattern of behavior and attitude displayed by our Lord and Savior Jesus Christ.

There is no greater honor or accomplishment on this earth than to become more and more like Jesus. Jesus Christ was the perfect model and example of godliness. He demonstrated what it means to have a mind that is constantly in tune with the goals and objectives of heaven. Unlike many of us, Christ did not allow the wickedness of the world, the fascination with the flesh or the deception of the devil to influence his thinking. Instead, Christ kept his mind sanctified, pure and focused on the will of God. This is what enabled him to say to his Father, "I glorified Thee on the earth, having accomplished the work which Thou hast given Me to do" (John 17:4). Jesus was qualified to make such a statement because he was completely faithful to his Father. He possessed a holy and righteous mind that kept him on course and compelled him to always choose his Father's will.

I ask you, Do you desire to overcome a defeated mindset? Do you wish to live above the level of mediocrity? Do you long to change negative messages in your mind that have hounded you since childhood? Do you want a mind that is sanctified, pure and focused on the will of God?

If so, you must begin by memorizing Scripture. You must spend time meditating on God's Word. And then you must mimic the life of Jesus as it is found in the Word of God. When we commit to practicing these three things, the quality of our thoughts will elevate. And when the quality of our thoughts is elevated, the quality of our lives will soar!

8 || You Are More Than
What You Have Become

Do you recall the Disney movie *The Lion King*? I certainly do. I must have watched the video version a dozen times with my kids. In the opening scene, King Mufasa, in grand fashion, presents his son, Simba, as the official heir to the throne.

Simba, the young lion cub, is full of confidence and promise. He worships and adores his father. Mufasa, in turn, is proud of his son and derives great joy from grooming Simba for greatness. In time Simba would ascend to the throne, taking his rightful place as king of the pride.

When Mufasa is murdered by his evil brother, Scar, Simba's world is shattered. What is worse, Simba is tricked into believing that he is responsible for his father's death. Confused and afraid, Simba runs away. He runs as fast and as far as his little legs would carry him. He runs away from his family, his heritage and his destiny.

For several years, young Simba lives in exile, aimlessly roaming through the jungles of Africa. Although he is heir to the throne of King Mufasa, Simba exists as a carefree, irresponsible vagabond who keeps company with a wart hog and a rodent! Simba is finally jarred back to reality when his father appears to him in a vision. In the vision, King Mufasa forces his son to face the truth. Mufasa's words to Simba are "You are more than what you have become. Remember who you are!"[1]

Of course we all realize that The Lion King is only make-believe. Yet in real life many of us, like Simba, are living in the jungles of spiritual exile. Although, we belong to the royal family of God, all too often we forget who we are. God has a wonderful plan for his children. But we cannot experience that plan when we roam through life as vagabonds, justifying mediocrity, nursing the wounds of rejection, disappointment, hurt or failure.

The truth is that, as children of God, we are joint heirs with Christ. We have royal blood streaming through our veins. We are destined for greatness. That is the truth! Yet when we believe the lies of the enemy that tell us that we are losers, we nullify the power of truth in our lives, and we reinforce the spiritual strongholds that defeat us and keep us imprisoned inside Satan's fortified wall of deception.

WHAT IS TRUTH?

Indeed truth is the first of the divinely powerful weapons that God has given us for the destruction of strongholds. It is the indelible imprint of truth in our minds that deletes the false messages of the world, the flesh and the devil—thus reprogramming our thinking with the kind of information that will set us free.[2]

Embracing truth is vital in the process that leads to personal transformation. But what is truth? Men have grappled with this question for ages. The dictionary defines truth as the quality of being true.[3] This explanation is adequate, but there is far more to the issue of truth than a simple academic definition. At the most fundamental level, truth has to do with what God has declared to be absolute.

Truth has little to do with our subjective opinions and standards, cultural and generational biases or even our theological persuasions. It has everything to do with the nature and character of God. God is the source of truth. God does not merely set a standard for truth; God is the standard. God did not simply create truth; rather God exudes out of his very being: absolute, objective, universal and constant truth—always.

In a sense truth is simply God's disclosure of himself. In a world of fluctuating values and relative standards, it is imperative that we learn to embrace what God has declared to be real and authentic. As an act of our will, we must adopt God's eternal values as the standard to which our attitudes and behavior conform. For this to happen, we must begin to see all of life and its many choices in the light of truth.

The primary vehicle through which God discloses truth to people today is the Bible. Jesus prayed, "Sanctify them in the truth; Thy word is truth" (John 17:17). The Bible is not on the same level as works produced by men such as Shakespeare, Plato, Alex Haley, or the founding fathers of our nation. No! The Bible is altogether different.

Although the Bible was written over a span of sixteen hundred years with over forty different writers, its author is God. Because God is the author, the words of Scripture have a divine dimension to them. The Bible is the only book in existence that is supernatural in nature. Contrary to some folk's perception, the Bible is not an "archaic book of stories." It is the inspired, infallible and inerrant Word of God.

Why is all this important? It is important because the Word of God is the single most effective instrument, in an arsenal of spiritual weapons available to us, to defeat the enemy and claim the victory in the fierce battle for the mind. Notice what the writer of the book of Hebrews says concerning God's Word:

The word of God is living and active and sharper than any two-edged sword, and piercing as far as the division of soul and spirit, of both joints and marrow, and able to judge the thoughts and intentions of the heart. (Hebrews 4:12)

This is a riveting passage of Scripture. It lets us know that the Word of God is not some dead commentary that merely offers an opinion on life. Instead the Word of God is alive and powerfully active! It motivates, inspires and energizes those who take its message seriously. But for those who trifle with God's Word, it condemns and executes. The Word of God is sharper than a two-edged sword; it cuts both ways. It is a weapon that gives life to those who believe and apply its truth; but for those who reject its light, the Word passes judgment.

SPIRITUAL WARFARE

In another section of Scripture, the apostle Paul writes, "And take . . . the sword of the Spirit, which is the word of God" (Ephesians 6:17). The context in which Paul is writing has to do with spiritual warfare. It is here that the apostle speaks of the armor of God. In the list of spiritual armor that the apostle Paul provides, there is only one offensive weapon mentioned. What is that offensive weapon? It is the sword of the Spirit, which is the Word of God! Let's take a closer look.

Paul begins this section of Scripture by saying:

Finally, be strong in the Lord, and in the strength of His might. Put on the full armor of God, that you may be able to stand firm against the schemes of the devil. For our struggle is not against flesh and blood, but against the rulers, against the powers, against the world forces of this darkness, against the spiritual forces of wickedness in the heavenly places. Therefore, take up the full armor of God, that you may be able to resist in the evil day, having done everything, to stand firm. (Ephesians 6:10-13)

There are several things that this passage teaches as it relates to the spiritual battle in which we are engaged. First, we are instructed to rely on the power of God and not on our own ability when confronted with the forces of darkness. Paul says, "Be strong in the Lord, and in the strength of His might." The fundamental truth that Paul is conveying to us is that we cannot compete with Satan.

The devil's intelligence, power of persuasion, spiritual perception and access to information is infinitely greater than our own. Satan is a skilled, experienced and ruthless destroyer of people's lives. Our pitiful human efforts to defeat him or defend ourselves against his calculated attacks are useless!

Too often I see misinformed and confused Christians assailing Satan in their own strength. Their passionate cries of rebuke, binding or casting out sound authoritative, but they have little power. Satan is neither intimidated nor impressed by our animated shouting, stomping and issuing of "spiritual" threats! Satan is an incredibly organized, resilient and focused foe. It will take far more than an emotional display to dampen his evil resolve.

Does that mean we do not have authority over the devil? That is not what I am saying. As Christians we do have authority over Satan. However the authority that we have is not based on our superior spiritual prowess; instead it is based solely on our position in Christ. Therefore our only hope of survival and ultimate victory in this spiritual battle is to depend not on our strength but on the strength of God.

THE ARMOR OF GOD

Next, we are instructed to come to the battle dressed in the appropriate attire for combat. "Put on the full armor of God, that you may be able to stand firm against the schemes of the devil." The word *stand* communicates a defensive posture and not an advancing attack. The word *scheme* in this verse describes the systematic strategies, cunning methods, tricks and deceptions of Satan.

Satan has a repertoire of clever plots that he uses to break us down and keep us in bondage. As Satan advances toward us, spewing out lies of deception, our most potent defense is to dress up in God's armor and stand firm on the truth of God's Word.

When we do this, Satan's assault on us is unsuccessful. We are able to walk away from his onslaught unmoved and victorious. The key is to dress appropriately for the attack. Apart from God's armor to protect us against Satan's bombardment we do not stand a chance!

Imagine a defensive lineman in the NFL showing up at the game dressed only in Fruit of the Loom underwear? Obviously he wouldn't last very long in the contest. Without the protection of his shoulder pads, kneepads, helmet and Nike shoes, one "pop" from an opposing player and he's counting stars.

Many Christians are showing up on the spiritual line of skirmish dressed only in underwear! Yet this need not be the case. God has provided protective gear for us. It is called the armor of God. And just as a football player needs protection against the aggression of the opposing team, we too need protection against the aggression and vicious attacks of Satan.

PEOPLE ARE NOT THE PROBLEM

Once Paul has expressed the importance of relying on the strength of God and wearing the protective armor of God, he then identifies the true enemy of our souls: Satan and his evil empire of demonic beings. Paul says, "For our struggle is not against flesh and blood, but against the rulers, against the powers, against the world forces of this darkness, against the spiritual forces of wickedness in the heavenly places."

In the pursuit of personal transformation, it is helpful to know that people (flesh and blood) are not the problem. Of course Satan uses other people to complicate our lives or to throw us off track, but the real adversary is Satan himself. Satan would have us believe that the conflict is taking place in the realm of the physical. When he is successful at diverting our focus away from himself and his structured government of demons, Satan is free to wage war against us unchallenged and often undetected.

Next, on the basis of who and what we are up against, Paul reiterates the tremendous need and urgency to protect ourselves against Satan and his demonic army. He says, "Therefore, take up the full armor of God, that you may be able to resist in the evil day, having done everything, to stand firm" (Ephesians 6:13).

Paul follows this urgent call to put on God's protective gear with a description of the various pieces of spiritual armor that God has provided.

> Stand firm therefore, having girded your loins with truth, and having put on the breastplate of righteousness, and having shod your feet with the preparation of the gospel of peace; in addition to all, taking up the shield of faith with which you will be able to extinguish all the flaming missiles of the evil one. And take the helmet of salvation, and the sword of the Spirit, which is the word of God. With all prayer and petition pray at all times in the Spirit, and with this in view, be on the alert with all perseverance and petition for the saints. (Ephesians 6:14-18)

The belt of truth. First on the list is the belt of truth: "Stand firm therefore, having girded your loins with truth." In preparation for battle, the ancient soldier of Paul's day wore a belt around his waist in order to tuck away the loose, sagging clothes that would be a hindrance in hand-to-hand combat.

Strapping on the belt meant tightening things up or pulling in all the loose ends before going into battle. Today many of our youth, particularly young men, consider it fashionable to wear sagging pants in a loose-fitting manner. Although I do not personally endorse this style of dress, it has become common and acceptable in our culture. Now, suppose boxing champion Oscar De La Hoya stepped in the ring wearing a loose-fitting outfit with sagging pants to fight an opponent. What do you think would happen? He'd probably get clocked! Why? The outfit would hinder and restrict his movement.

Unfortunately many Christians are being knocked out in the spiritual boxing ring because we have far too many loose ends in our lives. Just as the loose ends of an inappropriate outfit would hinder a boxer's performance, the loose ends of unresolved issues relating to personal integrity weigh the Christian down. Such potentially dangerous distractions hinder and restrict our spiritual movement toward maturity—and leave us open to satanic sucker punches.

Satan uses the loose ends in our lives to his advantage. When the apostle Paul says, "Gird up your loins with truth," he is saying that the spiritual belt that tightens up all of the loose ends in our lives is truth or truthfulness. It is our personal integrity and faithfulness to Christ that provides protection against the low blows of Satan. Paul is telling us to put on the belt of truthfulness. He is saying, "For your own protection, tighten up in the area of integrity and faithfulness!"

The breastplate of righteousness. Next on the list is the

breastplate of righteousness. The breastplate was a heavy piece of material that covered the soldier's torso, protecting vital organs such as the heart, kidneys and liver. Paul's meaning here is that, as believers, we have a natural, practical covering of protection when we are growing in our walk with Christ. When our hearts are filled with the righteous character of God, Satan is unable to deliver penetrating blows that will cripple us in our spiritual journey.

The gospel of peace. The third article of protective armor that Paul mentions is the gospel of peace: "Having shod your feet with the preparation of the gospel of peace." The soldier that Paul has in mind wore boots that were fitted with sharp cleats or nails on the sole. These shoes were designed to grip the ground and prevent the soldier from losing his footing when being attacked. It would have been extremely difficult for a soldier to focus on the battle if he was worried about slipping and sliding to the ground or losing his balance each time the enemy approached. His specially designed boots put his mind at peace.

Too often we are robbed of peace of mind, simply because we are not firmly rooted in our relationship with God. As a result of this spiritual insecurity, we slip to the ground of despair or lose our spiritual equilibrium whenever Satan challenges our faith. Peace of mind is a powerful defense mechanism against the advances of the devil.

Peace of mind is a byproduct of peace with God. The gospel shows us how to obtain this peace. When we have peace of mind as a result of standing firm on the truth of the gospel, we are able to keep our footing when under the attacks of Satan! Peace is what Christ gives us for the purpose of calming our hearts and minds, thus providing tranquillity and stability in our lives. Do you have peace of mind? If not, perhaps you have never understood the gospel of peace.

The shield of faith. Item number four on the list is the shield of faith: "Taking up the shield of faith with which you will be able to extinguish all the flaming missiles of the evil one." The soldier's shield was a very large piece of wood that was overlaid with linen, leather and treated with oil. The shield protected the entire body, particularly against airborne flaming arrows.

Paul paints a vivid picture here, depicting Satan's weaponry of temptation, disappointment, depression, disillusionment, defilement and defeat as flaming arrows aimed straight at the believer. What protects the believer against these satanic projectiles is the shield of faith—the believer's confidence and trust in God and his Word.

When we become the targets of Satan's air raid of deception, our trust in God is what extinguishes his fiery darts and renders such evil weapons harmless. But when we lack confidence in God and his Word, Satan's flaming arrows hit the mark, reducing to ashes our joy, peace, sense of purpose and resolve to pursue God's destiny for our lives!

The helmet of salvation. Fifth on the list of spiritual armor is the helmet of salvation. The head was always a primary target in combat. If a soldier was struck in the head during battle, usually it cost him his life. The helmet was designed to protect against such a fatal blow.

In spiritual battle, the satanic lies that produce doubt and discouragement are just as devastating to the mind of the child of God as bashing in the head of an ancient soldier. The assurance of salvation (simply standing on the truth that God will never leave us nor forsake us) serves as the protective head gear that guards our minds against such attacks.

The sword of the Spirit. Finally, after listing these five defensive articles of protective armor, Paul slips an offensive spiritual weapon into our hands: "And [take] the sword of the Spirit, which is the word of God." Paul had in mind a relatively small but sharp dagger that the ancient soldier used in battle, not only to defend himself against attack but also to take the offensive by initiating the attack. Without this offensive weapon in hand, ultimately, the battle could not be won.

In spiritual warfare, without the offensive weapon of the Word of God in our hearts, ultimately, the battle for the mind will not be won! Not only must we defend ourselves when under the attack of Satan, we must also take the initiative by proclaiming what God has declared to be true about us and our circumstances.

The Greek word used for *word* refers to a strategic word of truth from Scripture that is prompted to memory by the Holy Spirit and spoken by the believer at an appropriate occasion of testing or temptation. What the apostle Paul is saying to us is that uttering a powerful, strategic word of truth when confronted with demonic deception is like piercing the heart of Satan with a sharp dagger—he will quickly retreat!

It is clear from Scripture that the Spirit of God uses the truth of God's Word not only to expose us to the sin that is often hidden inside our hearts, but the Spirit also uses the truth of Scripture to expose the schemes that Satan uses to deceive us. Satan's whole game plan is dependent upon deception—his ability to trick us into believing a lie.

While the deceit of the enemy is powerful and convincing, it is weak in that it cannot withstand truth. We can cut through Satan's web of deception when we hide the Word of God in our hearts and speak the appropriate word of God to our circumstances.

IT IS WRITTEN!

Jesus, in his humanity, clearly understood this. When facing intense temptation in the desert, Jesus' strategy for victory was rooted in the utterance of the appropriate truth of God's Word. We see this in the Gospel of Matthew:

> Then Jesus was led up by the Spirit into the wilderness to be tempted by the devil. And after He had fasted forty days and forty nights, He then became hungry. And the tempter came and said to him, "If You are the Son of God, command that these stones become bread. But He answered and said, "It is written, Man shall not live by bread alone, but on every word that proceeds out of the mouth of God." Then the devil took Him into the holy city; and he had Him stand on the pinnacle of the temple, and said to Him, "If You are the Son of God throw Yourself down; for it is written, He will give His angels concerning You; and On their hands they will bear You up, lest You strike Your foot against a stone."
>
> Jesus said to him, "On the other hand, it is written, You shall not put the Lord your God to the test." Again, the devil took Him to a very high mountain, and showed Him all the kingdoms of the world, and their glory; and he said to Him, "All these things will I give You, if You fall down and worship me." Then Jesus said to him, "Begone, Satan! For it is written, You shall worship the Lord your God and serve Him only." Then the devil left Him; and behold, angels came and began to minister to Him. (Matthew 4:1-11)

To each of Satan's diabolical propositions, Jesus' response was consistent: "It is written." Jesus' rejection of Satan's lies rendered Satan's strategy powerless. But Jesus did not stop there. He went a step further. Jesus not only rejected Satan's lies, he also replaced Satan's lies with God's truth. Finally Jesus resisted further advances of the devil by dismissing him altogether. When in the midst of spiritual conflict we must follow Jesus' example. We must *reject, replace* and *resist!*

Reject. The Bible instructs us not to be ignorant of Satan's devices or schemes (2 Corinthians 2:11). Instead we are to reject the devil's attempts to trick us by appealing to God's truth. Satan is a liar. He cannot deal with truth. When we reject his lies with the appropriate Word of truth, his strategy begins to unravel.

Let me show you how this works. The next time Satan whispers lies of discouragement, defeat, guilt, failure or fear to your mind; say to yourself and to Satan:

"*I am* a child of God!" (Romans 8:16)
"*I am* redeemed from the hand of the enemy!" (Psalm 107:2)
"*I am* forgiven!" (Colossians 1:13-14)
"*I am* saved by grace through faith!" (Ephesians 2:8)
"*I am* justified!" (Romans 5:1)
"*I am* a new creation!" (2 Corinthians 5:17)
"*I am* a partaker of his divine nature!" (2 Peter 1:4)
"*I am* redeemed from the curse of the law!" (Galatians 3:13)
"*I am* delivered from the powers of darkness!" (Colossians 1:13)
"*I am* getting all my needs met by Jesus Christ!"
    (Philippians 4:19)
"*I am* strong in the Lord and in the power of his might!"
    (Ephesians 6:10)
"*I can* do all things through the strength of Christ!"
    (Philippians 4:13)
"*I am* more than a conqueror!" (Romans 8:37)
"*I am* the light of the world!" (Matthew 5:14)
"*I am* daily overcoming the devil!" (1 John 4:4)
"*I am being transformed by the renewing of my mind!*"
    (Romans 12:2)

Truth breaks the power of Satan's influence in our lives. When this occurs, we advance forward in the direction of liberation from the bondage of strongholds and stubborn habits.

Replace. Rejecting thoughts or suggestions that promote and reinforce negative patterns, without replacing those thoughts with appropriate truth from God's Word, is only fighting half the battle. It is not enough to say no to thoughts that originate from the world, the flesh or the devil. In order to destroy strongholds in the mind, we must aggressively replace destructive thinking with thoughts that emanate from God and his Word.

Replacing a mindset that feeds off the lies of the enemy, with a mind that is nurtured by the truth of God's Word, is the essence of what 2 Corinthians 10:4-5 means. In that passage Paul writes:

> For the weapons of our warfare are not of the flesh, but divinely powerful for the destruction of fortresses. We are destroying [rejecting] speculations, and every lofty thing raised up against the knowledge of God, and we are taking [replacing] every thought captive to the obedience of Christ. (2 Corinthians 10:4-5)

When I became a Christian in 1976, the refuse of worldly thinking had thoroughly contaminated my mind. Even as a believer, the mental garbage that littered my thoughts continued to hinder my spiritual growth and development. It wasn't until I adopted a vigorous plan to clean up my mind, through Bible study, meditation and Scripture memorization, that I was able to reject certain negative thoughts and replace those thoughts with God's truth. Of course mastering this discipline continues to be an ongoing battle; still, it was at that point that I began to make noticeable progress in my walk with Christ. Make no mistake; if we are to experience victory in the battle for change, saturating our minds with truth is non-negotiable.

Resist. Finally, not only must we reject satanic lies that influence our minds and replace those lies with God's truth, we must also learn to resist the devil when he approaches us in the first place. The Bible instructs us to: "Submit therefore to God. Resist the devil and he will flee from you" (James 4:7).

When we choose to enter into the presence of God, by filling our minds and hearts with his Word, we are able to resist the devil. Satan is like a roaring lion, roaming the earth, seeking unsuspecting or ill-equipped people to devour. When Satan is stalking us, remember it is not our smarts that fend him off. It is not our resources or our education that dissuades him. When Satan's ferocious roars send chills down our spines, it is the sword of the Spirit—the Word of God—that strikes fear in his heart and neutralizes his power!

REMEMBER WHO YOU ARE

Speaking of roaring lions, in the movie *The Lion King,* Scar's wicked scheme to take over Mufasa's kingdom almost succeeded. His diabolical plot to eliminate the competition nearly cost Simba, the legitimate heir to the throne, his life. The thing that turned it around was truth. Once Simba saw himself in the light of truth the seed of greatness exploded in his heart. No longer was he defeated in spirit or dominated by fear. Instead a sense of purpose flooded his soul, compelling him to fulfill his destiny.[4]

Are you defeated in spirit? Does fear dominate your life? Perhaps Satan has tricked you into believing that you are nobody, a loser, a mistake or a failure. Indeed he may have convinced you that your past is too dirty or that you have no future or destiny. Satan is a liar. You are somebody. You are a joint-heir with Christ, and God has a great purpose for your life. God's purpose is like hidden treasure—buried deep in the pages of his Word. When you dig into the Word of God, nuggets of truth will fill your mind with hope, vision and purpose.

The truth of God's Word is what sets us free. The truth of

God's Word is what opens our eyes to who we are in Christ. The truth of God's Word is what nurtures the seed of greatness inside us. The truth of God's Word is what causes the warrior in us to rise up to reclaim the territory that was stolen by Satan. It is the truth of God's Word that reminds us that we are more than what we have become!

9 || Who Do You Say I Am?

Earl was the custodian for the inner-city church in Washington, D.C., where our ministry was conducting a conference. Earl loved the game of baseball. More important, Earl loved to talk baseball to anyone who would listen. During breaks in the conference, Earl would show up at my table and take me on a verbal excursion down baseball's memory lane.

Listening to Earl relive the glory days of his baseball career was fascinating. He described in vivid detail the monster home runs, pitching wizardry and amazing catches that always, as he put it, "Worked the crowd into a frenzy!"

As I observed this man, I could tell that his janitorial wages left him struggling to make ends meet. But there was something else about Earl that concerned me. It was obvious from his conversation that he was stuck in the past and desperately trying to recapture a moment in time when he possessed a sense of significance.

In the midst of one of Earl's colorful flashbacks, I felt the urge to ask him where he stood with God. I was careful not to interrupt his flow; so I waited patiently for my opportunity. Finally after several minutes there was a break in the action. I quickly stepped up to the mound and whisked a fast ball of my own right down the middle of the plate. " Earl, if you were to die tonight do you know where you would spend eternity?" That question caught him off guard. Earl was not sure how to respond. I could tell that he was not used to talking about spiritual things. Earl was out of his league. Strike one!

I pressed on. "Earl, do you know that God loves you and has a wonderful plan for your life?" A suspicious glare hit me from the corner of his eye. Earl was uncertain about a personal God having a personal plan just for him. I could sense his skepticism. Under his breath he muttered, "Yeah, I guess so . . ." But he was doubtful. A swing and a miss. Strike two!

I was now winding up for the final pitch. I wanted Earl to see that, no matter how heroic he may have been on the baseball field, without Christ he was sure to strike out in the game of life. But just as I was about to deliver, Earl threw a wicked curve ball of his own. "Let me ask you a question," he said. "Do you believe that a person really went to the moon?" What?

I was not prepared for this tactic. My initial reaction was to laugh. After all, what possible connection does landing on the moon have with one's eternal destiny? It took a moment for me to regain my composure. I tried to get back on track, sharing the gospel from my little *Four Spiritual Laws* booklet. By law number three, I realized that Earl was serious about this moon thing. And he was determined to convince me that the whole episode was a hoax.

So there we were, in the basement of this inner-city church. I was trying to convince Earl of his need for Jesus, and Earl was trying to convince me that human beings never landed on the moon! Believe me, you had to have been there to appreciate the dynamics of that moment.

By the grace of God I got through my presentation of the gospel. I asked Earl if he would like to invite Jesus into his life. He paused and started rubbing his stubby, unshaven face. I could sense that Earl was uncomfortable. Finally after several moments, Earl whispered in his raspy old voice, "No, I'm just not ready to believe that." He got up and walked away. Strike three!

REJECTION OF TRUTH DOES NOT ALTER TRUTH!

Earl's refusal to believe God's Word was disturbing. But understand that his decision, as tragic as it was, did nothing to diminish the power of truth. Earl's rejection of Jesus Christ would only deepen the emptiness in his life.

There are many people in our culture like Earl—people who miss out on the benefits and blessings of God's truth simply because they choose to walk away from a relationship with God's Son. These people suffer from what I call a "truth deficient" mindset. A truth deficient mindset is a spiritual condition that creates skepticism and reluctance in a person when it comes to accepting and acknowledging the veracity of God's Word.

Unbelievers are not the only ones who suffer from truth deficiency. As Christians we, too, are vulnerable to succumbing to this spiritual problem. A truth deficient mindset for the believer is most likely demonstrated by a lack of faith. *Lack of faith* is really an expression of skepticism and reluctance to believe and appropriate the truth of God's Word. It is an indication that intimacy with Jesus Christ is missing in one's life.

It is crucial to understand that there is a direct correlation that exists between personal transformation and intimacy with Jesus Christ. Jesus is the living Word. Therefore the impact of truth in our lives will always be in proportion to the depth of intimacy that we have with Jesus Christ, the embodiment of divine truth.

ONLY ONE WAY

Jesus made the statement, "I am the way, the truth, and the life; no one comes to the Father, but through Me" (John 14:6). Not only is this statement by Jesus emphatic and definitive, it can be quite offensive to some. Often I am accused of being narrow-minded and intolerant because I tell people that Jesus Christ is the essence of truth and the only avenue whereby human beings may reach God.

"You mean to tell me that all these other religions are wrong?" they shout. "And all these sincere, good-hearted people who are not Christians are lost?" Yes! They are wrong, and they are lost not because of my opinion but because Jesus has defined truth. And the truth of Christ is absolute. You may choose to ignore or disregard the truth, but your disapproval does not negate its reality.

With the use of the definite article *(the)* in John 14:6, it is clear that Jesus is not suggesting that he is one of many options of truth or one of several expressions of truth. No! What Jesus is saying is that he is truth. He is not merely a conduit through which truth flows; he is the very origin, source and essence of truth!

Why is this important? It is important because lasting, significant change in our lives cannot occur outside the context of truth. And transforming truth is best understood and applied within the framework of an intimate relationship with Jesus Christ.

INTIMACY WITH CHRIST

Consider what Jesus says to a group of Jews who demonstrated belief in him as the Messiah and Son of God: "If you abide in

My word, then you are truly disciples of Mine; and you shall know the truth, and the truth shall make you free" (John 8:31-32). Again, Jesus says to his most trusted disciples, "If anyone loves Me, he will keep My word; and My Father will love him, and We will come to him, and make Our abode with him" (John 14:23).

In the final analysis, intimacy is what Christ desires most from us. This is because Jesus knows the value and power inherent in a relationship that is based on complete honesty, trust and transparency. It is also because Jesus knows that the application of biblical truth apart from spiritual, intellectual and emotional closeness with him is practically impossible. It is intimacy with Christ that produces an attitude of obedience in our hearts. And it is obedience to Christ that produces transformation in our lives!

A love relationship with Jesus Christ is vital in the process that leads to personal change. Yet it is incredibly difficult to love someone that we do not know. Therefore in order to develop the kind of intimate relationship with Jesus Christ that produces an obedient heart, we must first get to know him.

AND THE WORD BECAME FLESH

Who is Jesus Christ? Throughout history this question has created great confusion among men. Even while Jesus walked the face of the earth, there was speculation regarding his true identity. We see this in the episode recorded in Matthew 16. As Jesus and his entourage traveled along the dusty roads of Caesarea Philippi, Jesus raised the question: "Who do men say that I am?" His disciples answered, "Some say John the Baptist, others say Elijah, still others say Jeremiah or the prophet" (vv. 13-14). Wrong! Jesus is far greater than each of these extraordinary prophets.

Jesus did not become angry with the people for their spiritual ignorance concerning his identity. But he was interested in knowing where his disciples stood. "But who do you say that I am?" (v. 15). The concern of Christ has never been with the conjecture of the world, but with the convictions of his followers.

In response to Christ's inquiry, Peter, one of Jesus' original followers, declared, "Thou art the Christ, the Son of the living God." Jesus affirmed this declaration. He (Jesus) then clarified the source of Peter's knowledge by saying, "Flesh and blood did not reveal this to you, but My Father who is in heaven" (vv. 16-17).

John the apostle, another original follower of Christ, recorded this remarkable statement about Jesus: "In the beginning was the Word. And the Word was with God and the Word was God" (John 1:1).

This is one of the most powerful and controversial verses in the entire Bible. What this verse teaches about Jesus Christ may be shocking for some. To begin, the tense of the Greek verb that John uses for the word *was* literally means "had always been." What the apostle is saying is that in the deep recesses of eternity, before the creation of time, three things were true: First, the Word had always been; second, the Word had always been with God; and third, the Word had always been God.

Now I must admit, this verse can be a little confusing and unclear on the surface. But as we keep reading, all the confusion and cloudiness disappears. John says in that same chapter: "And the Word became flesh" (John 1:14). With that statement, the apostle John, under the inspiration of the Holy Spirit, identifies the Word (a Greek word meaning the "revelation of truth") to be Jesus. And in so doing, the apostle John declares Jesus Christ to be God.

"But I thought Jesus was born in the manger in Bethlehem," you say. That is true. Yet the Bible clearly teaches that Jesus' existence predates the nativity scene. According to John, before Mary or Joseph or Christmas, Jesus had always been. Not only that, but Jesus had always been with God. In fact, Jesus had always been God. "Well, what happened in the manger?" Jesus became flesh. He assumed a form he did not have in his eternal preexistence. Simply stated, God became a man—the flesh and blood revelation of truth!

But why in the world would Jesus—who is God—want to leave heaven and become a man? The answer to that question reveals the heart of the gospel message. You see, only as a man would Jesus be able to explain to us, in a way that we could understand, the inexhaustible love and holy character of the Father: "No man has seen God at any time; the only begotten God [Jesus], who is in the bosom of the Father; he has explained Him" (John 1:18).

Only as a man could Jesus fully relate to human weakness, failure and temptation. As a man Jesus legitimately felt the depth of human pain and suffering. Most important, however, is the fact that Jesus became a man in order to fulfill God's plan of redemption. He did so by going to the cross, shedding his blood, dying and rising from the dead on the third day so that you and I might experience forgiveness of sin. Had Jesus not become a man, the human race would be hopelessly lost, forever. The fact that Jesus took upon himself the nature of man (apart from sin of course) was God's way of showing his great love for humankind. Yet it is important to know that Christ's decision to clothe himself in human frailty did not negate the fact that he was God. Jesus did not abandon the eternal attributes of his deity. Rather Jesus chose to temporarily give up the prerogative to use those attributes while on earth.

Jesus is not just another man. He is not merely a good, moral teacher or prophet. The Bible clearly teaches that Jesus Christ is

Lord of lords and King of kings—uniquely God in human form. Developing intimacy with Jesus Christ then demands at least three things. First, it demands having a correct knowledge of who he is. Who is Jesus? He is God. Second, it demands having a correct response to that knowledge. How ought we to respond to God? We do so with reverence and humility, which involves confession and repentance of sin, an attitude of submission, and a heart of praise and worship. Third, it demands spending time in Bible study, prayer and meditation in the Word. Why? So that we might get to know him better!

As I have already mentioned, it is crucial that we resist the devil in order to tear down strongholds in the mind. While resistance is necessary, it is important to know that resistance apart from intimacy with Jesus Christ is futile.

A SOLID FOUNDATION

Note carefully the sequence of actions prescribed in James 4:7-8: "Submit therefore to God. Resist the devil and he will flee from you. Draw near to God and He will draw near to you." According to these verses, resistance is preceded by submission to God and proceeded by drawing close to God. Both of which are choices that lead to greater intimacy with God. Simply stated, our chances of successfully resisting the power of the enemy greatly increase when we submit to the authority of God in our lives and when we *linger* in the presence of God.

So often we are puzzled and frustrated by our lack of response to the Word of God. We read our Bibles. We study our Bibles. We are even taught the Bible by our pastors. Still, something is missing. There is no power in our lives. There is no change in our circumstances. In general, our level of response to God is pitiful. Why is this so? I believe it has to do with the fact that as Christians we often lack the foundation necessary for a life of power and obedience.

What do I mean by this? As Christians we fail to recognize that the Christian life is like a building project. We start with the basics and move from there. For example, when you are building a new house, before you can add that extra room, decorate the interior or install plush carpet, you must first establish a solid foundation that will support the structure and design that you have in mind. If you disregard this basic principle and proceed to erect the mansion of your dreams, it won't be long before the entire house crumbles before your eyes. Why? Because the house was built on shaky ground.

In the same way, the foundation for meaningful Christianity is intimacy with Jesus Christ. The prerequisite that Jesus sets forth as a condition for a life of obedience is intimacy: "If anyone loves Me, he will keep My word; and My Father will love him, and We will come to him, and make Our abode with him" (John 14:23).

Our efforts to maintain consistency of faith, trust and obedience to God apart from intimacy with Christ is like living in a mansion that was built on shaky ground—eventually it will break down and crumble!

If we do not love the Lord, we will not be motivated to live for him. It is that simple. Furthermore if we are not pursuing a love relationship with the Lord, we will not be able to sustain a desire to combat the negative influences that seek to dominate our minds and dictate our choices. In essence a lack of intimacy with Christ results in a minimal impact of truth in our lives.

On the other hand when we choose to draw close to Christ, we begin to experience the power of truth in a way that compels us to resist the overtures of the devil and to live in joyful obedience to the commands of our Lord and Savior. Our view of life will change. Amazingly, our view of ourselves will change too.

THIS JESUS STUFF AIN'T WORKING IN REAL LIFE!

I will never forget the time I met a young man named William. William lived on the tough streets of south central Los Angeles. His appearance told the story of his life. He was torn, battered and beaten down. It was obvious by the crazed look in his eyes that the pressures of life had pushed him beyond the edge.

I met this young man at a fast food restaurant. I was in between appointments with some pastors in the community. As I was about to sit down and enjoy a quick bite, I noticed someone approaching. Now to be honest, I was somewhat irritable that day and really not in the mood for company. William caught my eye, and I knew right away that I would not be dining alone.

With suspicion I watched this homeless person come toward me. As he drew closer I heard him mumbling something under his breath. He must have seen my Bible because when he finally reached my table, he looked me square in the eye and said, "I hope you can help me man . . . 'cause this stuff I've been hearing about Jesus and the church just ain't working in real life!"

I was taken aback by his statement. After hearing his story, however, I understood how he had reached that conclusion. William's life was like a giant jigsaw puzzle with hundreds of pieces scattered everywhere. It was a mess. He was a drug addict. He was jobless. He was homeless. He was hopeless.

Like so many, William had heard about Jesus, but he did not have a relationship with Jesus. He had tried church, but he soon discovered that it took more than religion to melt away the years of pain, confusion and anger that had hardened like spiritual plaque around his heart. Going to church had not changed William, it only frustrated him. That day I shared the gospel with William. By the grace of God, he prayed to receive Jesus into his life. Instantly, I witnessed a change in his countenance. I looked into his eyes and was amazed. The process of transformation was beginning to take place. I literally saw a glimmer of hope replace years of despair.

What made the difference? William was experiencing the power of truth through the power of a personal relationship with Jesus Christ. The living Word of God came alive and beckoned, "Come to Me, all who are weary and heavy-laden, and I will give you rest. Take My yoke upon you, and learn from Me, for I am gentle and humble in heart; and you shall find rest for your souls. For My yoke is easy, and My load is light" (Matthew 11:28-30).

William was tired; he was weary. Prior to this time, William had attempted to negotiate life on his terms and out of his own strength. Even though he had heard about Christ, he was not motivated to choose the way of Christ. But, oh, what a difference a glimpse of the Savior makes! Of course William would have to commit to the hard work (emotional healing, drug rehabilitation, etc.) necessary to sustain change. William was prepared to do this based on his new relationship with Christ—the one who could mend his broken life.

Now if only a glimpse of Christ can make such a profound impact in the life of a desperate drug addict, think what a lifetime of getting to know him can do for you! I ask the question: Are you intimate with the Lord? Your response may reveal the reason you lack peace, contentment or fulfillment in your life. Your answer may also explain your inability to experience personal transformation. If you said no to my question, then your need is clear. Draw near to God. Get to know Jesus.

A common reason why we are unable to break free of strongholds in our lives has to do with the fact that intimacy with Jesus Christ is missing. William was a prime example of this. For years Christ had been edited out of his world. As a result, William endured a painful life of bondage to addiction, hopelessness and a host of other dysfunctions.

As seasoned Christians, we, too, are unable to dismantle the strongholds that keep us down when we edit Christ out of our lives. In my own experience I notice that certain negative patterns I struggle with tend to crop up and resurface more frequently when my walk with Christ is not as intimate. On the other hand, the more intimate I am with the Lord, the more I am able to tap into his power. It is Christ who gives me the strength I need to rise up from the ashes of despair and failure to become the person that God designed me to be.

Indeed, intimacy with Christ infuses us with supernatural power. That is why, when we feel helpless to change or to break the power of a debilitating habit, we must run! Not from our problems but straight into the bosom of Jesus! For it is in the intimate presence of the Lord that we find the strength needed to win the battle for change.

10 || Hey God, Can You Hook Me Up?

In chapter four I told you about my goal as a kid to play basketball in the NBA. When my middle school coach tossed me a basketball, he gave me a dream. I pursued that dream with a passion. What I didn't tell you was that the same coach who gave me the dream of playing professional basketball, gave me something else that almost became my worst nightmare—an introduction to pornography.

On many occasions after a grueling workout at the gym, Coach and I would relax by sitting in his basement flipping through the pages of *Playboy, Hustler* or some other hard core "skin" magazine. At the time I had no idea how risky or stupid this was. I was only a kid. And I trusted my coach. Neither did I anticipate the struggles I would face later in life as a result of exposing my mind to such graphic images. I do understand, however, that I was fortunate. You see, I never made it to the NBA, but I came dangerously close to becoming addicted to pornography. What saved me from the clutches of that world of seduction was God's response to a simple prayer, "Lord, deliver me from this stuff."

As I whispered those words, the Lord heard the desperate cry of my soul. He moved on my behalf, changing the desire of my heart. I began to lose the appetite for pornography. Before long I was able to walk past news stands and adult bookstores without being tempted to "sneak a peek." I was delivered! God responded to my cry for help and changed the direction of my life.

Your struggle may not be with pornography. Whatever your situation, you need to know that prayer works. And God designed prayer specifically with you in mind. Prayer is the second divine weapon available to us for the destruction of strongholds. This may sound simplistic or trite to some, but I know from personal experience that prayer works. Yet it is not my experience alone that validates prayer; ultimately it is the testimony and witness of God's Word.

PRAYER WORKS

In the Bible we catch a glimpse of God's eagerness to act on behalf of people, families and even nations, simply because someone prayed. For instance in the book of Acts we read that a group of believers prayed, and in spectacular fashion God delivered the apostle Peter from a prison cell in Jerusalem, where he sat on death row awaiting execution (Acts 12:5-11)

In the Old Testament we read of Hannah, a middle-aged Jewish woman who suffered from infertility. For years she felt shame and disgrace for not being able to provide children for her husband, Elkanah. When she took her case before God, he heard her prayer, and Hannah gave birth to a son (1 Samuel 1:1-20). That boy's name was Samuel (which means "heard of God" or "because I have asked him of the Lord"). Samuel became the last of the judges of Israel and a great prophet and spokesperson for God. There is more!

Nehemiah, a Jew, was a government official on the payroll of the pagan king of Persia. When he learned of the terrible condition of his homeland, he prayed. In response God gave him favor before the king. Not only was Nehemiah able to mobilize his people to rebuild the walls of Jerusalem, God also caused the pagan king Artaxerxes to finance the entire project (Nehemiah 1:1—2:10).

Elijah the Tishbite was a prophet who, at times, struggled with deep depression and discouragement. Yet when he prayed, the windows of heaven were shut tight; there was no rain on the earth for three-and-a-half years! Again he prayed, and at the end of the three-and-a-half year period, the floodgates were opened, and the rains came pouring down (James 5:17-18).

When the fires of wrath and judgment scorched the streets of Sodom and Gomorrah, God dispatched an angel to escort Lot and his family to safety. Why did God do this? Because Abraham prayed. And, in response to Abraham's prayer, God spared his nephew Lot (Genesis 18:22-33). I could go on citing examples from the Bible, but I think you get the point: prayer works.

Perhaps you are not convinced that prayer works. Maybe you are saying to yourself, "Those were Bible characters, they don't count. Of course God answered their prayers. But what about today? Does prayer work for ordinary people like me?" The answer is *yes!* You see, prayer was never designed to be a benefit reserved for a select group of people who lived in a certain period in history.

Prayer is not restricted to Bible characters or so-called professional Christians, such as pastors, missionaries or praying grandmothers. On the contrary! Prayer is a privilege that is available to all God's children. And it is designed to work today—for the ordinary person like you and me.

How does prayer work? No one knows for sure. It is a mystery that has never been solved. Yet our lack of understanding of how prayer works does not negate the fact that it does work.

As I write this chapter I am watching the NBA playoffs on television. The Indiana Pacers and New York Knicks are in a dogfight for the Eastern Conference title. Now I admit, I do not understand the technology that makes it possible to transmit a live basketball game from Madison Square Garden in New York into my small bedroom in Atlanta.

In fact, I don't understand how television works, period. Nevertheless each time I press the power button on my remote control, I expect results. I don't know how it works, but I believe that it works.

In a similar sense, when it comes to prayer, I may not understand the theology that explains how God, who is in heaven, transmits relevant, timely answers to prayer into my personal reality on earth. I do not know exactly how it works; yet when I pray, I expect results. I believe that it works.

Do you believe that prayer works? One reason why people do not believe in prayer is because of common misconceptions concerning prayer. For example, some believe that prayer is nothing more than a spiritual American Express card—designed to give them whatever they want. These people go around claiming all sorts of outrageous things that have nothing to do with God's will.

Others believe that when they pray it is simply a time when God joins them at the bargaining table. These people feel that if they negotiate hard enough or long enough or if they say just the right words, eventually, God will change his mind about their requests and strike up a deal.

Still others see God as a stingy celestial tycoon who is sitting in heaven with a scowl on his face, dreading to share his blessings or to hear the concerns of his people. These false ideas about prayer do not produce results and often cause people to lose confidence in God.

Prayer is not our ability to manipulate God or to "out-slick" him into giving us things that he did not mean for us to have. Nor is prayer our ability to change God's mind about something that is not his will. Certainly God is not a stingy or reluctant God. Our prayers do not irritate him. Instead, prayer is God's way of changing our hearts, our minds and our perspectives—so that our wills are being brought into alignment with his will and purposes (Matthew 26:36-42). We have all heard the statement, "Prayer changes things." I am convinced that what prayer changes most is our stubborn self-will!

CONDITIONS FOR POWERFUL PRAYER

Prayers that touch the heart of God, causing him to move on our behalf, require that we meet certain conditions. When they are fulfilled, these conditions create the atmosphere for a dynamic journey of asking and receiving from God. What are the conditions for powerful prayer? Having faith, abiding, praying in Christ's name and praying according to God's will. Let's briefly examine each of these.

Faith. In the Gospel of Matthew, Jesus unleashes a scathing rebuke on his disciples. The reason for the denunciation was the disciples' inability to help a desperate father whose son was possessed by a demon. This man, like any father, was concerned for his boy. When he spotted Christ's disciples, he assumed that they had the right stuff to cast out the demon. The father was terribly disappointed in the disciples' performance.

When Jesus arrived on the scene, the father wasted little time exposing the failure of Christ's followers. Irritated by this man's announcement, Jesus cries out, in what appears to be righteous exasperation, "O unbelieving and perverted generation, how long shall I be with you? How long shall I put up with you? Bring him here to Me." At the Lord's command, the demonic spirit hastily abandons his human living quarters (Matthew 17:17-18).

Upon witnessing this incredible display of power, the disciples came to Jesus privately and asked why they could not cast the demon out. Christ's response was remarkable: "Because of the littleness of your faith; for truly I say to you, if you have faith as a mustard seed, you shall say to this mountain, 'move from here to there,' and it shall move; and nothing shall be impossible to you" (Matthew 17:20).

Wow! Did you notice what Jesus said? If you have faith as small as a mustard seed you have the ability to rearrange the mountains in your life—and nothing shall be impossible to you! I get excited when I read passages like this because it lets me know that through faith I can overcome obstacles in my life. It also reveals that I do not need to possess great quantities of faith to be effective—as long as I have the proper quality of faith.

What do I mean? In this incident with the demon-possessed boy, it is clear that the failure of the disciples was due to unbelief, which in this case literally means little faith. The phrase "littleness of your faith" comes from two Greek words, one meaning little and the other meaning faith. When you combine the two words the idea becomes little faith or littleness of faith.

This Greek word does not convey the concept of complete absence of faith. Therefore it is safe to conclude that Christ's disciples did possess some measure of faith. The problem was that the little faith that they had was deficient, in that it was lacking in *quality*. Tapping into God's power, which is available through prayer, is impossible apart from the proper quality of faith.

The word *faith* is the Greek word that means belief, trust or confidence. While some struggle with the concept of faith, or make it more complicated than it is, the Bible teaches that biblical faith is simply trust and confidence in God. When there is a consistent, unwavering attitude of trust and confidence in God (the object of faith) then the little faith that we have is sufficient in quality and has the potential to explode into tremendous power, accomplishing extraordinary things.

Faith is not a deep confidence in our own abilities. Nor is biblical faith an esoteric concept, emotional feeling or positive confession that we must exert in order for God to grant our requests. The object of faith is not faith itself. But biblical faith is simply belief in God; it is taking God at his word and adjusting our lives accordingly.

Just as the mustard seed was tiny, but had the amazing ability to grow up into a blossoming plant, faith that is consistent, steady, expectant and directed toward God, even though small in quantity, has the potential to grow up and remove mountains. This is what I mean by the proper quality of faith. Jesus says when we possess this kind of faith, nothing shall be impossible for us.[1]

Abiding. A second condition for powerful prayer is abiding. Jesus said, "If you abide in Me, and My words abide in you, ask whatever you wish, and it shall be done for you" (John 15:7). Again, this is one of the great promises of the Bible! The implications of this verse are staggering.

When Jesus made this statement he stood in the shadows of Calvary's cross. For three-and-a-half years, he had poured himself into the lives of the men he selected to carry out his mission. Now, in the final hours of his earthly ministry, Christ felt it necessary to reiterate and explain to his chosen those things that were most important.

The principle of abiding was one of those things. This truth would be essential for his disciples to grasp in order to successfully carry out their tasks. The basic point of the lesson was spiritual productivity. Christ was teaching his disciples that, to be productive and fruitful in life and ministry, they must learn to depend totally and completely on him.

The analogy that Christ uses to explain this principle is the natural union that exists between a branch and the vine. This comparison describes what ought to be the natural relationship between Christ and the believer. Just as a branch cannot bear fruit apart from the vine, neither can the believer bear fruit apart from Christ.

The word *abide* basically means to remain. When the word *abide* is followed by the preposition *in,* as is the case in this verse, the complete meaning is to abide in or remain vitally and intimately connected to someone or something. Jesus is saying in this verse that, for believers to have fruitful, productive lives, we must remain in vital, intimate contact with himself (Christ), the source of life.

Christ explains how this is done in John 15:7 when he says, "And My words abide in you." Abiding in Christ is inseparable from experiencing deep fellowship with Christ through reading, studying and obeying his Word.

Dr. Curtis C. Mitchell, in his book *Praying Jesus' Way,* says, "To abide in Christ is to be so adjusted to Christ as to have uninterrupted fellowship with him. It is remaining in reliance upon him, of being open to receive from him the spiritual vitality for successful fruit bearing."[2] The essence of abiding is to enjoy uninterrupted fellowship with the Lord, which should be the natural state for the believer.

It is unnatural for us as Christians to live independent of Christ, drawing upon our own strength and reserves. Just as the natural condition of the branch is to receive its sustenance from the vine, the natural state of the child of God is to receive spiritual sustenance from the Lord.

When we abide, or live, in uninterrupted fellowship with Christ, we are linked to him in such a way that we receive spiritual nourishment, energy and strength from his life. In a real sense, Christ's life becomes our life. This is what the apostle Paul meant when he wrote these words: "I have been crucified with Christ; and it is no longer I who live, but Christ lives in me" (Galatians 2:20).

I am convinced that we have weak prayer lives, and we miss out on so much from God simply because we are disconnected from Christ. It is shameful; but it is true for many of us that, when we should be abiding in Christ, all too often we choose to break away from the Lord to do our own thing. It is precisely at this point that our lives lose focus and power.

When we choose to live independent of Christ, our spiritual vitality wanes. Our ministries wilt. Our prayers are without direction, stale and lack spiritual authority. Ultimately when we cut ourselves off from Christ, our lives dry up and wither—leaving us discouraged and frustrated.

You can see how abiding in Christ influences our prayers. When we abide in Christ and his words abide in us, a vital connection is established. Christ's desires become our desires, and our prayers are not the dead, dry rituals that reflect our own self-serving agendas. Instead our prayers become alive and powerful, expressing the very heart of Christ. To be linked to Jesus in this way guarantees that our prayers will be on target—and, when our prayers are on target, we can expect to receive what we wish.

Praying in Christ's name. The third condition that the Bible talks about for a life of powerful prayer is asking in Jesus' name.

Jesus said, "And whatever you ask in My name, that will I do, that the Father may be glorified in the Son. If you ask Me anything in My name, I will do it" (John 14:13-14; see also 15:16; 16:23-24).

By now we all should be bursting at the seams with excitement and expectation! What we are able to accomplish through prayer seems limitless in its possibilities and privileges. We need only meet certain conditions to claim God's promises. So far we have seen what a small amount of the proper quality of faith can do. We have also discovered the benefits of abiding in Christ. But what is this praying in the name of Jesus?

First let me tell you what it is not. We have all heard people recite ridiculous prayers that had absolutely no basis in Scripture. Yet they boldly and confidently cap off their petition by stating, "In Jesus' name, I pray. Amen!" Does this mean that God will automatically answer their prayers? Do these people meet the condition set forth in John 14:13-14? Hardly!

To pray in Jesus' name goes far beyond mumbling a few words at the end of a prayer. It is not some magic potion or spiritual rabbit's foot that injects our requests with power. The idea of praying in Jesus' name is not based on some fixed formula; instead it is rooted in the identity and authority of Christ. It is approaching the Father on the basis of Christ's person, presence and position.

In our culture, a name carries little significance in relation to the nature of a person. This was not the case in the first century. In that culture, a name was often associated with a person's character, disposition, personality and even destiny in life. In his book *Experiencing God* Dr. Henry Blackaby says, "A Hebrew name described a person's character or nature. The name was closely associated with the person and his presence. Thus to call on one's name was to seek his presence."[3]

When Christ said, "Ask in My name," his disciples were not puzzled or perplexed about what he meant. They understood that Jesus was giving them VIP access to the Father, not on the basis of who they were but on the basis of who He was. To the disciples, asking in Jesus' name meant acknowledging Christ's person, presence and position—including all the privileges, status and authority that belongs to him.

It is interesting that Jesus gave this instruction in anticipation of his death and resurrection. Christ knew that upon completion of his mission, spiritual warfare would intensify and the enemy would focus his major attacks on the twelve disciples. To offset this diabolic strategy, Christ gave his men a weapon that would stop the enemy in his tracks. This weapon was borrowed authority! The only way the disciples could access this authority was through praying in the name of Christ.

As the exalted King of kings and Lord of lords, Christ knew that all authority in heaven and earth would ultimately rest with him. It was in anticipation of this coming reality that Jesus assured his disciples that he would endorse their prayers with his authority when they petitioned the Father in his name.

When we approach the Father on the basis of the authority of Christ, we have the endorsement of heaven on our side. What an awesome privilege!

Recently I received a traffic ticket for driving above the speed limit. I was not driving recklessly, but I was traveling a bit fast. The officer that stopped me was not very impressive physically. In fact he appeared terribly out of shape. I am sure I could have overpowered him and drove on about my business, had I decided to do so. But the thought never crossed my mind. Why? Because I recognized the authority that was behind his badge. Although this cop did not personally have the physical prowess to do much, the entire city of Atlanta had his back!

When we pray in the name of Jesus, we are in essence acting as officers of the kingdom, seeking the goals and objectives of the King. Although we may lack spiritual prowess to accomplish much on our own, when we represent the King, the entire kingdom of heaven has our backs!

According to God's will. The final condition for powerful prayer is asking according to God's will: "And this is the confidence which we have before Him, that, if we ask anything according to His will, He hears us. And if we know that He hears us in whatever we ask, we know that we have the requests which we have asked from Him" (1 John 5:14-15). Actually this incredible promise is not a condition in the same sense that faith, abiding and asking in Christ's name are. Rather, praying according to God's will is the overarching principle that governs and qualifies all prayer as being legitimate requests of God.

Let me explain. A request for God to do something is valid in so far as the request falls under the umbrella of God's divine will. Suppose it is not God's will that I become the president of the United States of America. Then for me to ask for the presidency would be an invalid request, and to begin raising funds "by faith" to launch a presidential campaign would be presumptuous (not to mention stupid).

In order for a request to qualify for an affirmative answer from God, the request must fall in line with God's will. For many people this truth is a difficult pill to swallow. Yet to ignore this reality is to live in denial. We have all experienced the pain, disappointment and even confusion that come as a result of not receiving that for which we so desperately prayed and hoped.

Many people have claimed healing for their loved ones, only to watch them die. Untold numbers of people have prayed to be raised from their beds of affliction, only to remain in the clutches of disease, terminal illness or in the confines of a wheelchair.

Many have confessed material blessings and prosperity, only to plummet into financial ruin and despair. Thousands of would-be mothers have begged God for children, only to go through life childless. People have prayed for jobs, promotions, relationships, houses and cars; yet they did not receive what they asked for.

How can this be? It is so because God is not obligated to do what we ask, if what we ask does not fit in with his plan and purposes for our lives. No matter how hard we pray or how right a thing may seem to us, God will not sanction the petition or grant the request if it is not his will.

As a parent I try to say yes to my kids more than I say no. I do this because I don't want Kimya, Whitney, Brian and Courtney to remember Dad as a mean old grouch. There are times, however, when they will ask for something that I know is not good for them. When that happens, my response to their request is negative.

What is interesting is that no matter how firmly I say no, invariably they will come back again and again using different tactics and strategies in attempts to break me down. Their goal is obvious. They want to persuade me to change my mind and give them what they want. Usually I am able to hold my ground. But there are times when I allow myself to be manipulated into giving in to their wishes.

At times God will say no to our prayers when those prayers do not line up with his goals for our lives. When we strategize, pout, whine, beg and make false promises to God in an attempt to get our way, we are using manipulation. We are saying, "God, I know what is best for me; give me what I want!"

Another reason why our prayers go unanswered has to do with our own evil desires. When God created us, he built into our human makeup the freedom to make choices. We are not sophisticated robots that have been programmed a certain way. Nor are we puppets dangling from a string that reaches to heaven! We are moral beings with the freedom of choice. Unfortunately the exercising of our freedom is not always devoid of sinful motives. God does not respond to our prayers when the motive behind our prayers is selfish. The Bible says, "You ask and do not receive, because you ask with wrong motives, so that you may spend it on your pleasures" (James 4:3). Nor will God force others to do that which we have prayed for, if the purpose of their hearts is to choose evil.

Yet when we pray according to God's will, we choose to submit to God's wisdom, timing and direction for our lives. As a result we experience growth and develop maturity. In such circumstances we learn what it means to depend on God. We learn what it means to release our personal anxieties and trust God to work out his purposes in our lives.

Fortunately God is not like us. He cannot be manipulated into acting in a way that is inconsistent with his character. God will always do what is best for us—even when it is painful or unpleasant. To demand from God what God is not willing to give only creates frustration, disillusionment and disappointment, which ultimately leads to unbelief.

GOD IS SOVEREIGN

There are times when God receives greater glory from our lives by forcing us to patiently wait for his answer. Other times God is honored when we endure suffering or when we journey through the valley of brokenness or the fires of testing. We do not always understand or appreciate this process. Yet when we pray we must recognize that it is God's sovereign prerogative to do as he pleases or as he sees best.

When we approach God with an attitude of humility, seeking

his will and not our own, our prayers will reach a whole new level of power and effectiveness. We will no longer insist on having things our way. Instead we will learn to wait on God. We will learn to trust in God. We will learn to obey God. Most important, we will learn to pray as did Jesus: "Not as I will, but as Thou wilt" (Matthew 26:39).

What is it that you wish for today? Do you wish to destroy a stronghold in your mind that's holding you back? Do you wish to be free from drugs? Do you wish to be free from lust? Do you wish to be free from anger? Do you wish to be free from the guilt of your past? Do you wish to become a loving husband or wife? Do you wish to become all that God wants you to be?

These things are God's will for you! Have faith in God, abide in Christ, ask in the name of Jesus, seek God's sovereign will and *pray.* God is ready to respond!

11 || Someone Help Me, Please

The final divine weapon that God has given us to destroy strongholds is the Holy Spirit. Now this weapon is powerful! When we understand how God's Spirit operates in our lives, we will become like a one-person spiritual wrecking crew, utterly demolishing the fortresses that the enemy has erected in our minds!

The Holy Spirit is the power source for the Christian today. Yet even in our so-called enlightened age, there remains a tremendous level of apprehension on the part of believers to access this power. I am convinced that ignorance and negative experiences account for a large portion of this apprehension.

HIT BY THE HOLY GHOST!

When I was growing up in Indiana, all of the kids at the neighborhood church I attended were terrified of the Holy Spirit. We were afraid because it seemed that this invisible force arbitrarily and randomly selected certain people to "hit" and caused them to do strange things against their wills.

It was like clockwork. Whenever the preacher reached the

emotional climax in his sermon or the choir member hit that "soulful" note, the little old ladies would start jumping, shouting, moaning, dancing, flinging their arms or frantically pacing the aisles. When asked what prompted this weird behavior, their response was always the same, "I couldn't help it . . . the Holy Ghost hit me."

The whole thing seemed spooky to me. I did not wish to be "hit" by the Holy Ghost. So I stayed clear of the usual targets, and I kept my eyes open just in case I spotted something coming my way!

Looking back I realize that my fear of the Holy Spirit was based more on personal ignorance than anything else. And while I am sure that many of those church members who were hit on a regular basis were sincere, their emotional expressiveness did little to communicate accurate theology concerning God's Spirit.

So what, or better yet, who is the Holy Spirit? And how does the Holy Spirit help in the battle for change? Many scholars have written volumes on this important topic. In fact there is so much material in bookstores today about the Holy Spirit, it hardly seems necessary for me to add to the already voluminous library of information.

Therefore the goal of this chapter is not to debate the various doctrinal perspectives or to give an exhaustive theological analysis of all the issues related to this topic. Instead the objective here is to emphasize the significance of the Holy Spirit's role in empowering the believer to consistently make godly choices and to experience radical transformation in his or her life. The three areas of the Holy Spirit that I will focus on are: the Holy Spirit's presence, person and power.

THE HOLY SPIRIT'S PRESENCE

Does the phrase "May the Force be with you" sound familiar? If you are a *Star Wars* fan it should. In this epic adventure of good versus evil, the Force is a reservoir of unlimited power, waiting to be tapped for the good of the galaxy. This invisible presence enables the good guys to operate far beyond their natural abilities in an effort to triumph over evil.

In the *Star Wars* movies, Luke Skywalker and other Jedi warriors are locked in a life and death struggle with the bad guys to save the galaxy. The bad guys, known as the Dark Side, are powerful and ruthless adversaries led by mysterious figures such as Darth Vader.

As a *Star Wars* fan, I have discovered a certain pattern in the plot. Whenever the good guys are in trouble, no matter how hopeless the situation appears or how close to disaster they come, in the end all is well. Why? Because the Force is with them!

As Jedi warriors, these men have a special calling on their lives to save the galaxy. But they are able to fulfill their calling in so far as they rely on the Force, which is always present with them and in them.[1]

Of course *Star Wars* is not real. Yet it beautifully illustrates the spiritual truth concerning the presence of the Holy Spirit in the life of the believer. In the same way that the Force is present with the Jedi warriors, assisting them to fulfill their calling, the indwelling presence of the Holy Spirit is our constant companion, assisting us to accomplish the tasks to which God has called us. A major distinction, however, is that the Holy Spirit is not an impersonal force but a personal being, as we will see later in this chapter.

AN INVISIBLE HELPER

In his final discourse, shortly before departing from earth, Jesus informed the disciples that their days of basking in the glory of his physical presence were over. There would be no more leadership retreats with the Master, no more speaking tours that attracted thousands. Life for these men was about to change dramatically.

Jesus said, "And I will ask the Father, and He will give you another Helper, that He may be with you forever; that is the Spirit of truth, whom the world cannot receive, because it does not behold Him or know Him, but you know Him because He abides with you, and will be in you" (John 14:16-17). At the time Christ spoke these words, the only thing standing between him and his exit from the planet was the cross—which drew closer with each passing moment. This disturbing information that he shared left the disciples grief-stricken and uncertain about the future.

Sensing their pain and insecurity, Jesus sought to comfort his disciples by affirming his love for them personally and by confirming his commitment to them as a team. Jesus did this by vowing to send a helper. This helper would, in a sense, take up where Christ left off. He would be a companion closer than a brother. And although his presence would not be visible to the naked eye, this helper would, in fact, more effectively aid the disciples in fulfilling their mission than Christ himself. How was this possible?

First, the physical laws of the universe restricted Jesus while in his humanity. During his earthly ministry Jesus had a physical body. Therefore he could not personally indwell those who followed him. The helper, on the other hand, is noncorporal in nature. That means he does not possess a body comprised of material substance. As a result, laws and principles of physics do not apply to him.

The Holy Spirit possesses the capacity to be everywhere at once. He is not restricted to a particular location at a specific time. Therefore the Holy Spirit was able to be with the disciples corporately, as well as to indwell them individually. The concept of being indwelt by the Holy Spirit was completely new and radical.

Up to this point in history, the Holy Spirit only visited or came upon a person for a specific purpose and for a limited period of time. Once the objective for which the Spirit came upon a person was fulfilled, the Holy Spirit departed.

Now Jesus was promising his disciples that, upon his departure, the Spirit's availability and presence would no longer be occasional or temporary but personal and permanent. This new development, which was scheduled to happen on the day of Pentecost, would be a tremendous benefit to the believer.

Second, the invisibility of the Spirit would help to strengthen the disciple's faith. In the world, most people have to see a thing before believing. This is not the case in God's economy. God designed life to be a faith journey. God often calls us to put our trust in the invisible and the yet unfulfilled. When we do this, and we see things happen that have no rational human explanation, we tend to have greater confidence and boldness in God's presence and power.[2]

A friend of mine who for years struggled with alcoholism tells of his "miraculous" deliverance. After countless, dismal attempts at kicking the habit, he finally just gave up. Discouraged and defeated, my friend resigned himself to a life of misery. When he committed his life to Christ, the inexplicable happened. The desire and taste for alcohol left.

What cold turkey, AA and other programs could not do, God by his Spirit accomplished in an instant. Today, my friend's faith is strong, and he continues to walk with the Lord. Of course God does not work in the same way for everyone. For most, kicking an addictive habit is a process that often requires time, professional counseling and accountability. Still, with the presence of the Holy Spirit helping at each step, hope for success is greatly enhanced.

The English word *helper* in this text is a Greek word that means one who comes alongside. This designation reveals a significant aspect of the Holy Spirit's ministry. Essentially, the Holy Spirit's job on earth is to glorify Christ. One way this is done is by coming alongside the child of God, assisting us to become effective witnesses for Jesus Christ.

In Acts 1:8 the Bible says, "But you shall receive power when the Holy Spirit has come upon you; and you shall be My witnesses." Obviously being a witness for Christ involves sharing our faith verbally with other people. But it goes beyond that. A verbal testimony and articulation of what we believe has little influence if our lives are a mess! If what we say does not match up to how we live, we actually do more damage to the kingdom than good.

As witnesses, we need supernatural power to effectively communicate the gospel to others. We also need supernatural power to live out the principles of the gospel in our marriages, on the job, in the classroom, on the college campus, in our relationships with others and in all aspects of our daily lives. This is where the indwelling presence of the Holy Spirit comes in.

Just as the Force was present with the Jedi warriors at all times, the invisible, indwelling presence of the Holy Spirit is always there for the believer. We may not be able to see, touch or smell him through our physical senses. But there is never a time in which he is not there. For the Christian, from the time of conversion, the presence of the Holy Spirit is with us and in us always.

THE HOLY SPIRIT'S PERSON

In John 14:16-17 there is a common, but inconspicuous, word that gives us even greater insight into the Holy Spirit. It is the word *another*. This unassuming word reveals the true nature of the Holy Spirit's person.

Jesus said, "I will ask the Father and He will send you another Helper." In the English language, the word *another* simply means something else or someone else. But the Greek language is far more colorful and expressive than English. In Greek, the word that is translated *another* literally means another of the same kind or another of the same quality. With the use of this word, Jesus is saying that the nature of the Holy Spirit is equal to that of his own.

In basketball, when the superstar of the team is sidelined from the game (due to injury, fatigue or foul trouble) another player from the bench replaces him. This is commonly known as a substitution. Usually the sub is not as good an athlete as the superstar player. If the clutch player does not return to action, the team may lose momentum or even the game. The reason for this is that the substitute's performance is usually inferior to that of the superstar.

In the minds of many, when the topic of the Holy Spirit comes up, he is thought of as a spiritual bench-warmer! He's like a second string player who belongs on the sidelines. Such erroneous perceptions of the Spirit of God must be rejected. The Holy Spirit is not a celestial water boy or substitute. On the contrary, the Bible teaches that the Holy Spirit, in essence and substance, is equal to Jesus. And since Jesus, in essence and substance, is equal to the Father, guess what category that puts the Holy Spirit in? That's right—the superstar, slam dunk, God category!

Jesus is assuring the disciples that the coming of the Holy Spirit would in no way compromise the integrity of the movement of Christianity. There would be no momentum swing. The Holy Spirit would not be a disappointment, downgrade or step backward. Instead the Holy Spirit would be a person of tremendous power. He would be a person of the same caliber and in the same class as Jesus himself.

Theologically we would say that the Holy Spirit is the third person of the Trinity, coequal to God the Father and God the Son. This may be a difficult concept to understand; nevertheless it is true. The two primary lines of reasoning that the Bible uses to affirm this truth focus on the Holy Spirit's attributes and activities.

THE HOLY SPIRIT'S ATTRIBUTES

The Bible teaches that the Holy Spirit is omnipresent. That means there is not a location in the entire universe where the Spirit of God is not present. Just as God the Father dwells everywhere at once, the Holy Spirit has the same ability to be everywhere, concurrently and simultaneously. In the words of King David, "Where can I go from Thy Spirit? Or where can I flee from Thy presence? If I ascend to heaven, Thou art there; if I make my bed in Sheol, behold, Thou art there. If I take the wings of the dawn, if I dwell in the remotest part of the sea, even there Thy hand will lead me, and Thy right hand will lay hold of me" (Psalm 139:7-10).

The Bible also teaches that the Holy Spirit is omniscient. That means the Holy Spirit possesses all knowledge, or he is all knowing: "For the Spirit searches all things, even the depths of God. For who among men knows the thoughts of a man except the spirit of the man, which is in him? Even so the thoughts of God no one knows except the Spirit of God" (1 Corinthians 2:10-11).

A third attribute that the Holy Spirit possesses is omnipotence. To be omnipotent means to have unlimited power. It is to be all-powerful: "And Jesus returned to Galilee in the power of the Spirit" (Luke 4:14). The word *power* in this verse is a Greek word that refers to the supernatural, miraculous, abundant ability of God.

Each of these attributes—omnipresence, omniscience and omnipotence—are characteristics that describe deity. The Holy Spirit possesses these attributes; therefore we can conclude that the Holy Spirit, while distinct in person, is in essence and substance equal to God.

THE HOLY SPIRIT'S ACTIVITY

It is also clear from Scripture that the Holy Spirit is aggressively involved in what God the Father and God the Son are doing in the world and in the lives of people. For instance, the Holy Spirit creates:

> In the beginning God [*Elohim*, plural] created the heavens and the earth . . . and the Spirit of God was moving over the surface of the waters. (Genesis 1:1-2)

The Holy Spirit empowers:

> But you shall receive power when the Holy Spirit has come upon you; and you shall be My witnesses both in Jerusalem, and in all Judea and Samaria, and even to the remotest part of the earth. (Acts 1:8)

> And when they had prayed, the place where they had gathered together was shaken, and they were all filled with the Holy Spirit, and began to speak the word of God with boldness. (Acts 4:31)

> But I say, walk by the Spirit, and you will not carry out the desire of the flesh. (Galatians 5:16)

The Holy Spirit is called the Spirit of truth, or literally Spirit of the truth. This title refers to the Holy Spirit's ministry of teaching and guiding the believer. Every word, thought and idea that the Holy Spirit imparts to and impresses on the believer's heart consistently flows out of the deep wellspring of eternal truth. As such, the Spirit of the truth accurately guides people into the reality of God's will. Too often people make poor choices for their lives, claiming to have been led by God. They are mistaken. The Holy Spirit cannot lead a person down the wrong path.

Some time ago a Christian brother informed me of his wife's plans to file for divorce. I asked why. His answer startled me. Apparently my friend's wife, a professed believer, felt that the Spirit of God was leading her to abandon her husband along with their children.

Of course this was absurd! The Holy Spirit would never lead in such a way. The fact that this dear woman felt it necessary to terminate her marriage cannot be disputed. Who or what prompted those feelings is quite a different matter. The Spirit of truth cannot contradict the revealed principles, ordinances, commands or truths of Scripture; to do so would be a violation of his own character and integrity.

The Holy Spirit teaches. "Now we have received, not the spirit of the world, but the Spirit who is from God, that we might know the things freely given to us by God, which things we also speak, not in words taught by human wisdom, but in those taught by the Spirit, combining spiritual thoughts with spiritual words" (1 Corinthians 2:12-13).

The Holy Spirit guides. "But when He, the Spirit of truth, comes, He will guide you into all the truth" (John 16:13). In Acts 5 the apostle Peter confronts the deceit of Ananias and Sapphira. He asks Ananias, "Why has Satan filled your heart to lie to the Holy Spirit?" Then he adds, "You have not lied to men, but to God" (Acts 5:3-4).

Let there be no mistake, God the Holy Spirit is a rational, active being. He operates in the realm of the supernatural. We cannot see him with our eyes, but we can see the results of his work. When we speak of the Holy Spirit we are speaking of God!

THE HOLY SPIRIT'S POWER

A very important household appliance to have when keeping a clean house is a vacuum. A vacuum cleaner is designed to keep unwanted dirt and grime from ruining the carpet. To use one of these machines is easy enough. You simply pull it out of the closet, plug it into the electrical socket and let it do what it does best: clean!

But what would happen if, one day, when you decide to clean the carpet, you follow your normal routine except you forget to do one thing: plug in the vacuum? I don't have to tell you what will happen, you already know: absolutely nothing! You may have a new Kirby, Dirt Devil, Hoover or any other brand of machine. It wouldn't matter. Unless it is plugged into the power source, the vacuum is useless.

Are you aware that the Holy Spirit is the power source for the Christian? When we are plugged into the Holy Spirit, we are empowered to do what Christians are designed to do best: glorify Christ. But when we are out of the socket, we are powerless. Our educational background, ministry experience, spiritual giftedness or doctrinal distinctive makes little difference. When we are not connected to the power source, we are like a Kirby vacuum that someone forgot to plug in.

This is a serious matter. When we understand and appropriate the power that is available to us through the Holy Spirit, our lives will radically change forever. In fact I am convinced that the solution to just about every problem, issue or struggle we face in this life is rooted in a decision to live under the controlling influence of the Holy Spirit.

I realize that is a strong statement. But the apostle Paul writes: "But I say, walk by the Spirit, and you will not carry out the desire of the flesh" (Galatians 5:16). This is one of the most liberating verses in the Bible. Once we fully grasp the meaning of this verse we will never be the same.

The word *walk* (or *live*) here is a present imperative. It means to keep on walking. The idea is that, as we continue to live under the controlling influence of the Spirit, we will not (because we cannot) be manipulated or deceived by the world, flesh or the devil to choose a path that is contrary to the will of God. Remember the Spirit of the truth will always accurately guide you into the perfect will of God. That's his job!

So what Paul is saying to us is that the powerful influence of the Spirit overrules the negative influence of the flesh. He is saying that choosing to live consistently under such godly domination and direction automatically cancels out the power of any stronghold that Satan may have in our lives.

THE FRUIT OF THE SPIRIT

When we choose to walk by the Spirit, God initiates a work in our hearts whereby spiritual fruit is produced in our lives. "But the fruit of the Spirit is love, joy, peace, patience, kindness, goodness, faithfulness, gentleness, [and] self-control" (Galatians 5:22-23). The fruit of the Spirit does not come from us. Human ingenuity or effort does not manufacture it. Instead the seed of this fruit is sown by supernatural activity.

Although we have the responsibility to cultivate the seed through Bible study, prayer, renewing the mind and other spiritual disciplines, the fruit belongs to the Spirit. And as such, it is the Spirit who labors in our hearts and minds, effecting a radical metamorphosis in our character.

The fruit of the Spirit is not an apple, orange or banana. No! The fruit that the Spirit produces is a transformed character. This is one of the ways in which we are empowered. We do right because we are right. The more mature the fruit, the more consistent our behavior, attitudes and actions. The Spirit-filled life *guarantees* victory over sin.

In an audience of several hundred missionaries, Dr. Bill Bright, the founder and former president of Campus Crusade for Christ made an astonishing remark. He said that in forty years as a Christian, he has never been "defeated" by the enemy or by sin. Now that's a profound statement! I must admit, when I heard this, my initial reaction was skeptical. I thought, *This man is living in la-la land if he thinks he never sinned!* Of course Dr. Bright was not implying that he was sinless. He was stating, however, that in forty years he had not succumbed to the temptation to linger in sin, or to practice it habitually.

As Dr. Bright went on to explain the principles of the Spirit-filled life, things began to click in my mind. By the conclusion of his presentation, I realized that Dr. Bright wasn't in la-la land; I was, along with countless others who had allowed the enemy to beat us down.

Dr. Bright understood that at the point of temptation a crucial decision had to be made. He would either attempt to handle the moment in the power and energy of the flesh, which meant certain failure. Or he would respond in the power and energy of the Spirit, which always leads to success. It all really boils down to a moment of decision.[3]

From God's perspective, there is not a legitimate reason for the child of God to live or linger in defeat. Will we face challenges? Yes. Will we have problems and concerns? Of course! Will there be times when we stumble and fall? Absolutely! But these things should not break us down. God has put at our disposal the power of the Holy Spirit as an incredible spiritual resource. When we appropriate this resource in our lives, victory is most assuredly ours. This was Dr. Bright's secret to a life of power and victory.

THE SPIRIT-FILLED LIFE

In the book of Ephesians the apostle Paul writes, "And do not get drunk with wine, for that is dissipation, but be filled with the Spirit" (Ephesians 5:18). In this verse we have the mandate for walking by the Spirit, or what Dr. Bright refers to as the Spirit-filled life. What is important to understand is that God never gives a mandate without also giving the means to fulfill the mandate.

So how is a person filled with the Spirit? Or what does a person need to do to plug into this tremendous power source? The answer to these questions is amazingly simple. You need only keep four words in mind. They are *influence, obedience, repetition* and *faith.*

Influence. I am sure you have seen someone who was intoxicated from drinking alcohol. A few of the tell-tale signs are slurred speech, loss of coordination, gregarious jesters and a host of other behaviors that are probably not part of that person's normal personality. If the person has really had a few too many and becomes what we call "sloppy drunk," the behavior can be quite obnoxious, even dangerous.

Now the thing about alcohol is that when too much of it gets into the human system, it exerts a controlling influence on behavior. It impairs judgment, lowers inhibitions and often causes a person to act in ways that are out of context with their character. For instance a person who is an introvert and normally shy, when intoxicated, may become loud and boisterous. Such a person can quickly go from being a wallflower at a gathering of people to the proverbial life of the party.

When the Bible says be filled with the Spirit, it literally means to become intoxicated—not with wine, but with the consumption of the Holy Spirit! It means allowing the Spirit of God to get into our system, thus exerting a controlling influence on our behavior. When this happens we will find ourselves doing things that are uncharacteristic of our personalities, conditioning or established habits. Things such as: expressing love toward others when our normal tendency is to be critical, or experiencing joy in our hearts when our normal tendency is to allow our circumstances to create a situation of despair, or having patience and inner peace as opposed to anxiety and worry.

The Spirit of God desires to be the dominant influence in our minds. When we allow him to be so, he takes control of our lives, dictating our behavior, attitudes, our motives and actions for the good. My question to you is this: When was the last time you were intoxicated—not from alcohol, but from the consumption of the Holy Spirit?

Obedience. When the apostle Paul says, "Be filled with the Spirit," he is writing in the imperative mood, which means that he is actually commanding the Ephesian Christians to be under the controlling influence of the Spirit. To be filled with the Spirit is not a nice suggestion or option that we can take or leave. Being filled with the Spirit is an apostolic command, which comes directly from God.

When we choose not to be filled with the Spirit, it is disobedience! The consequence of such a choice is a powerless, lukewarm and impotent spiritual life. There is no question about the direct correlation that exists between our ability to overcome issues, deal with problems, cast down strongholds or conquer sin, and our decision to be filled with the Spirit. The first step to accessing the Spirit's power is an attitude of obedience.

Repetition. Not only is the apostle Paul writing in the imperative mood, but he is also communicating in the present tense. In other words being filled with the Spirit is not a one-time event, but it is a continuous, repeated experience. A literal translation of this verse could read, "Be being filled with the

Spirit." Of course this sounds strange, but the idea makes plenty of sense.

When you pay your gas bill in December, you cannot expect that one payment will cover your utility costs through June. It would be nice if that were the case, but we all know it does not work that way. The power is available, but if you wish to have uninterrupted service, you must continue to make payments each month.

In the same way, the Holy Spirit's power is available to us at any given moment. But we must decide to access this power each day in order to successfully meet the various and unexpected challenges of life. Just as one payment will not supply a house with power indefinitely, one Spirit-filled experience cannot be expected to sustain us throughout the Christian life! If we wish to experience victory consistently, then we must access the power of the Spirit on a continuous basis.

A fresh filling. Eric is a new Christian. Prior to his conversion, Eric struggled with a serious drug addiction. Now, as a new believer, Eric is trusting God for deliverance. Eric has been clean for two weeks, but it's Friday night and an old friend drops in to visit. Unaware of Eric's decision to follow Christ, the old friend reaches in his pocket, pulls out a bag of drugs and spreads them on the table.

At this point Eric is faced with a choice. He can either compromise his new commitment to serve Christ and pursue the urge to get high, or Eric can call on the Lord to give him supernatural strength to say no.

On this occasion Eric makes the right decision and calls on the Lord. The Holy Spirit empowers Eric to overcome the temptation. Eric walks away clean. This all happens on Friday night. On Saturday night, as Eric thinks about how close he came to relapsing, another friend shows up. He, too, reaches in his pocket and pulls out an assortment of drugs.

Again Eric is faced with a choice as he finds himself tempted to slip back into his old habit. Now this is the question: Will Eric's decision on Friday night guarantee his victory on Saturday night? The answer is no! In order for Eric to gain the victory a second time, the same process that led to his deliverance on Friday must be repeated again on Saturday. He must call on the Lord for a fresh filling with the Holy Spirit.

The same is true for you and me. We must get into the habit of calling upon the Lord each day, each moment, for a fresh filling with the Holy Spirit.

Your issue may not be with drugs. It may be learning to cope with the pain of past abuse. Or it may be that your spouse walked out on you, and you now find yourself submerged beneath the flood of loneliness, guilt and uncertainty. Perhaps your struggle is with uncontrollable anger. It could be that depression is your constant companion.

Whatever your personal struggle or challenge, remember that a moment-by-moment, fresh filling with the Holy Spirit will empower you to make choices that lead to God's solution to your problem.

Faith. Finally, we are filled with the Holy Spirit when we appropriate the filling by faith. What do I mean? The fact that we are commanded to be filled with the Spirit is an indication that God fully intended for us to experience this provision for power. Otherwise God simply could have made it optional or restricted the filling to a few super-saints. God did not do this. Instead God decided to make it a requirement and prerequisite for all Christians in order to be successful in life.

I appreciate Dr. Crawford W. Loritts's insight on this point. In his book *A Passionate Commitment*, Dr. Loritts makes this observation:

We are filled with the Spirit by faith. It is not a matter of beg-
ging or pleading with God to fill us with his Spirit. He is not trying to tease us or hold out on us. He wants to give us freely and
lavishly the power and joy we need to live the Christian life—
because we are filled by faith, we should not depend upon our
feelings. We may or may not feel anything. As long as we have
met God's requirements we can claim—by faith—God's promise to fill us.[4]

The promise that Dr. Loritts is referring to is found in 1 John
5:14-15: "And this is the confidence which we have in Him,
that, if we ask anything according to His will, He hears us. And
if we know that He hears us in whatever we ask, we know that
we have the requests which we have asked from Him." God will
fill us with the Holy Spirit when by faith we ask him to do it. It's
really that simple.

Of course we disqualify ourselves from being filled with the
Spirit when we harbor attitudes of rebellion, sin or unrepentant
hearts. But if we are right before God, we can be confident that
when we ask to be filled, God will do it. He promised!

God's desire and plan for us is that we experience victory in
our lives. God's provision of power that enables us to live victorious is the Holy Spirit. When we cry out to God for strength and
help in the battle for change, we must be prepared to make a
choice to live under the controlling influence of the Holy Spirit.

We must be prepared to respond to God's command to "be
filled with the Spirit" with an attitude of obedience; we must
seek his power on a continuous basis, and we must receive his
provision by faith.

When we do these things, we plug into the greatest power
source of the universe, the Holy Spirit. To be empowered by the
Holy Spirit means one thing: *victory!* With the help of the Spirit
of God, it is only a matter of time before we break free of the

strongholds that keep us in bondage. Through the power of the Holy Spirit, we will become the dynamic witnesses of the risen Lord that God designed us to be!

12 || Say That Again

Someone once asked the question, how do you eat an elephant? The answer: one bite at a time! My question is, how do you implement change in your life? The answer: one step at a time. In fact if you are like most people, you appreciate information in bite-sized chunks so that you are able to chew on the information, swallow and digest it without choking. What's more, if the information you are chewing on is tasty or nutritional, you probably would want a second helping. With that in mind, this chapter is sort of a second plate, a recap in bite-sized chunks of the six crucial steps that must be implemented in order to experience change.

Remember that change is a process. It usually does not happen overnight. Following these steps does not mean that all of your problems will disappear. It does mean, however, that you will taste the goodness and faithfulness of God. And that alone makes the effort worth your while. Let's revisit the essentials.

STEP 1: MAKE THE DECISION

The first bite that takes a chunk out of stubborn habits and debilitating attitudes and behavior is a decision. Decisions, more than anything, determine the degree of change you will experience in your life. It is in the moments of decision that you set into motion the events and circumstances that define your life.

STEP 2: DEAL WITH THE SIN IN YOUR LIFE

Next, you must chew on the fact that a sin-nature plays a major role in your inability to make right choices. Remember that Adam and Eve's failure in the garden fundamentally altered our nature. Originally people had a built-in tendency to respond naturally and instinctively to God. That was our nature. But after the fall, things radically changed for the worse. Depravity invaded our hearts, and our very nature became sinful.

Today the human heart is far from being naturally and instinctively responsive to God. In fact it is quite the opposite; from birth our hearts are naturally and instinctively rebellious, indifferent and apathetic toward God.

It is precisely due to this sinful heart condition that we struggle so desperately to make right choices for our lives. In our natural state, we are alienated from God and exist in passive or active rebellion against God. This state of alienation and rebellion destroys our resolve to obey God, thus leaving us impotent to make choices that are consistent with God's divine will.

In addition we must resist the temptation and tendency to shift the blame in an effort to escape the consequences of our sinful choices, attitudes and behavior. To see change occur in our lives, we must do three things to deal with sin.

Acknowledge. First, you must acknowledge it before God. The journey that leads to healing and deliverance from the power and dominance of sin begins with a step in the direction of God. God wants to transform our lives, but transformation cannot occur apart from acknowledging our spiritual failure and inadequacy before him.

God already knows our hearts, but he wants us to admit that we have a problem that is too big to handle on our own. God is waiting for us to stop denying the reality of sin's power in our lives and over our ability to make right choices. When we do this, we are agreeing with God; and when we agree with God, we put ourselves in a position to be helped by God. Until we acknowledge the presence and power of sin in our hearts, we will continue the practice of sin in our lives.

Ask and accept. Second, you must ask for God's forgiveness and accept God's cleansing. God is willing, eager and able to cleanse your heart through the forgiveness of sins. It matters not the attitude or behavior; when we are ready to come clean before God, he is eager to open the windows of heaven and shower us with his cleansing power.

Aggressive action. Finally, you must take aggressive action against the sin in your life. You must declare war on sin. When God reveals sin in your life, whether it is an attitude, action, thought or habit, you must immediately choose to turn away from the sin and toward God. This response to sin is known as the act of repentance.

Confession apart from repentance leads only to self-deception and creates a false sense of progress in the quest for change. When we take aggressive action against sin through a consistent pattern of confession and repentance, we grow closer to God. When we grow closer to God, we gain greater access to his power. Each day becomes a new opportunity to do the right thing. With each godly choice, strength is renewed, hope is restored, and we begin to believe that change is possible.

STEP 3: CHANGE YOUR PERSPECTIVE

After you have made the decision to change and have dealt with sin, you must digest the significance of perspective. Perspective determines priorities, which in turn dictate choices. In the battle for change, it is imperative that you develop a perspective that will propel you closer to God as opposed to selfish goals and objectives.

When we peer at life through the lens of the temporal, our choices will reflect the priorities and values of this world. We will pursue things that cater to personal interest and ambition. But this world is not our home. Heaven is where we are headed. Therefore we should not think and live as though we are bound to the temporal. Instead, the eternal values of God should shape our perspective, our priorities and choices. When this happens, ultimately the choices that we make will guide us into the center of God's will.

Maintaining the right perspective also helps us to respond properly to the challenges of life. We will never be able to control all the variables in life that come our way. Certain things will happen to us that are beyond our influence and ability to manipulate. While we cannot always control what happens to us, we can always control our response to what happens. Perspective is the key.

STEP 4: IDENTIFY STRONGHOLDS

Fourth, you must recognize that a spiritual stronghold may be at the root of your problems. Now, this bite may leave a bitter taste in your mouth because it has to do with the enemy of our souls. Yet awareness of the fact that, as Christians, we have an adversary who plays mind games with us is very important.

Satan is bent on keeping us immersed in the mire of negative thinking. Often we repeat the same old patterns of behavior, even though we know such behavior is harmful. We do so because of what's happening inside our heads.

When we are aware of the negative patterns of thought that are burned in our minds, dictating our choices and triggering dysfunctional behavior, we are better able to apply spiritual truths and principles necessary to fight the enemy and dismantle those strongholds that hinder change.

STEP 5: CHANGE THE WAY YOU THINK

Fifth, you must swallow the fact that change begins with the way you think. There is a raging battle taking place in our minds. In order to change the way we behave, we must first change the way we think. Victorious living demands victorious thinking. A major reason why we live defeated lives is because we lock ourselves into a defeated mindset. We must change the way we think by bringing our minds into consistent, meaningful contact with the Word of God.

When we memorize the Word of God, meditate on the Word of God and mimic the character of God as it is revealed in the Word of God, we give the Holy Spirit ammunition to sanitize our thinking from the pollution of the world, flesh and devil. How a person thinks determines how a person behaves.

STEP 6: DESTROY STRONGHOLDS IN THE MIND THROUGH THE USE OF DIVINE WEAPONS

The sixth and final bite-sized chunk has to do with spiritual warfare. You must chew on the truth that God has not abandoned you to fight the battle for change on your own. You have at your disposal divinely powerful weapons specifically designed to destroy the strongholds that lock us into negative patterns of thinking and behaving. These divine weapons are the power of truth (which is the Word of God), the power of prayer and the power of the Holy Spirit.

The power of truth. On the authority of God's Word, you must reject, replace and resist the lies of the enemy. Satan is a liar. He cannot deal with truth. When you speak against his lies with the appropriate Word of truth, Satan's strategy begins to unravel. Whenever Satan whispers lies of discouragement, defeat, guilt, failure or fear to our minds, we must quote the Word of God. Truth breaks the power of Satan's influence in our minds. It is the truth of God's Word that reminds us that we are more than what we have become.

The power of prayer. Prayer is a privilege that is available to all God's children. And it is designed to work today—for the ordinary person like you and me! Prayer is not our ability to manipulate God into giving us things that he did not mean for us to have. Nor is prayer our ability to change God's mind about something that is not his will. Instead prayer is God's way of producing change in our lives, so that our wills are brought into alignment with his will and purposes. It is true that prayer changes things, but the thing prayer changes most is our stubborn self-will.

The power of the Holy Spirit. Through the indwelling presence and in-filling power of the person of the Holy Spirit, we can effectively dismantle the strongholds in our minds that prevent us from becoming the people God designed us to be. We tap into the power of the Spirit when we choose to consistently live under his controlling influence, with an attitude of obedience and a heart of faith. The Holy Spirit is the power source for the believer. Apart from his supernatural empowering, our ability to effectively make choices that lead to personal transformation is nonexistent.

So there you have it. The anatomy of change in bite-sized chunks. As you chew on this information be sure to make up your mind to persevere to the end. Transformation is possible, but you must hang in there. I once heard someone say that it was by perseverance that the snail made it into the Ark. Things might seem slow and tedious. Don't quit! Keep on stepping! Persevere! With each step you are moving closer to your transformation.

As we approach the final pages of this book, I would like to rap things up by talking about the ultimate choice. Of course I am referring to the decision to follow Jesus Christ wholeheartedly and without reservation. In reality this is the most important decision we can make. It is out of the decision to follow Christ that we discover true meaning and purpose. From this decision we learn to appreciate and apply the spiritual disciplines that help us sustain change in our lives.

I Just Want My Talk!

Some time ago I visited my hometown of Fort Wayne, Indiana. It was a fantastic trip. I spent a lot of time with friends and relatives, staying up all night laughing, talking and just reminiscing about the good old days. One particular evening I noticed a friend of the family who was acting strangely.

He was irritable and moody and quiet all evening. After watching him sulk for a while, I decided to find out what was bothering him. "Is everything all right?" I asked.

In a flat tone he responded, "Not really."

"Well, what is it that's bothering you?" I followed.

With that question my friend tore right into me. "I'm disappointed in you, Raymond," he said. "You have been home several days now, and you have not even come over to my place to visit." I sat quietly as he continued. "Usually when you visit, you make it a point to drop by, to see how I'm doing and talk to me about the Bible. Why not this time?"

I thought about his question for a moment, and then out of curiosity I responded, "Does this mean you are finally ready to surrender your life to Christ?"

He shot a baffled look my way and retorted, "I didn't say all that . . . I just want my talk!"

I cannot help chuckling each time I think of that incident. But the disturbing truth is that in our culture many of us enjoy being around Christianity as long as we do not have to practice Christianity. We appreciate good Bible teaching and preaching. Songs of praise and worship touch us. Yet like my friend, we are not serious about our spiritual walk. Instead we just "want the talk!" Too often we are content to be in the vicinity of God, without ever experiencing the power of God to change our lives or circumstances.

Today more so than any other time in the history of the church we have access to biblical resources and tools that are designed to help us grow as Christians. On any given day of the week we have the option of attending a Christian conference, workshop, seminar or revival. The obvious goal of these Christian gatherings is to motivate us to develop a deeper walk with the Lord.

In my opinion the church is inundated with information. Yet I have discovered that no matter how much information we digest, apart from the application of the information, we will remain unable to move beyond the issues that render our lives stagnant.

Still, somehow we are being deceived into thinking that exposure to truth is synonymous with experience and power. And so, day after day, week after week, month after month and year after year we go through the motions of Christianity absorbing truth without ever experiencing change.

We occupy the pews of the great churches of this nation. We even possess a tremendous wealth of knowledge and facts about the Bible. But my question is, What good is an intellectual library of biblical facts if those facts do not translate into changed lives? I am sad to report that I meet far too many Christians today whose knowledge of the Bible is impressive, yet they live under the insidious cloud of spiritual impotence, never able to rise above the challenges of life.

Please understand that just because we attend church on Sunday morning does not necessarily mean that we have made a commitment to Jesus Christ or biblical Christianity. We may be a church leader, a Sunday school teacher or even a pastor. No matter what our role in the church, the fact remains that proximity to truth does not translate into transformation of character.

In order to experience significant growth and development in our lives, we must be willing to get off the roller coaster of indecision and make the ultimate life choice. And that choice is a total and radical commitment to follow Jesus Christ!

A TRUE DECISION CALLS FOR COMMITMENT

A decision is not really a decision until it produces a commitment to a particular course of action. For example, you may say, "I made a decision to quit smoking," or "I made a decision to lose weight and get in shape." You may say, "I made a decision to pray one hour each day." But if there is no commitment to action, then you have not truly made a decision. You have simply entertained some good ideas. A true decision is a commitment to a particular course of action.

As Christians, in the quest for change, the course of action to which we must commit, is a passionate pursuit of Jesus Christ. Jesus said, "If anyone wishes to come after Me, let him deny himself, take up his cross, and follow Me" (Matthew 16:24). That, my friend, is the ultimate invitation from Christ, and it demands the ultimate decision from you and me! It is a call to commitment. And like a sharp razor, this call pierces through the shallow misconceptions and erroneous assumptions that we have concerning a life of commitment.

Immediately Christ's words dislodge us from the comfort zone of complacency and compel us to examine the depth of our personal devotion to him. A deeper probe into this verse reveals that what Jesus is demanding from his disciples is really one momentous, life-changing decision that is sustained by a radical commitment to a particular course of action.

In other words the fundamental decision is to pursue Christ. But what validates the decision is a commitment to a life of self-denial, a willingness to suffer and a total surrender to Christ's leading. We cannot honestly claim to be followers of Christ if we are not willing to do what he says. At the core of New Testament discipleship is a commitment to do and to be exactly what Jesus Christ says. Ultimately it is not what we say that validates our decision to follow Christ; it is how we live.

Several years ago Donna came to me with tears in her eyes. By the look of things I could tell that something was really troubling her. I asked what was wrong, to which she responded, "I can't take it anymore . . . I need to be home." Well, this was a hot topic for us, and I knew where the conversation was going.

Donna was pregnant with Whitney, our second child, and she sensed God was leading her to quit the job and become a homemaker. I disagreed. I tried to be sensitive to Donna's feelings, but all I could think of were two things: *the mortgage payment!* . . . *the car note!*

We talked about it for a while, and then I said, "Let's pray." We both got on our knees and poured our hearts out to God. We finished praying, and immediately I told my wife to quit her job. Why the sudden shift on my part? God had made it clear to us that this was his will! What about the mortgage payment? What about the car note? Those were no longer my problems. My responsibility was to follow Christ. Christ's responsibility was to provide for our needs.

At the time I had no idea how that one decision would set into motion a series of events that drew us closer to God and eventually led us into full-time Christian work. But that is exactly what happened! God's will for our lives began to unfold once we made the decision to trust him—and to follow him regardless of where it may have led.

Now I am not suggesting that you run out and quit your job or that you join the mission field. That would be more along the line of presumption and not faith. I am suggesting, however, that God often starts the process of revealing his will for our lives at the point of a faith decision that we make to follow him.

What does this have to do with your personal transformation? Everything! You see, Jesus is calling out to you right now. He is whispering the words "Follow me." Do you hear his voice? It is soft and gentle. Yet there is power in his tongue. He is saying, "Your life can be different." He is speaking to that empty place in your heart: "There is hope. You can experience a sense of purpose and direction." Jesus is saying, "You can experience breakthroughs in your life, marriage, relationships, ministry and finances." He is saying, "You can experience changes in your circumstances." He is saying, "Follow me."

Do you hear his voice? Understand that there is nothing you can do to satisfy the deep longing in your soul if your will is not inextricably linked to the will of God. There is nothing you can find in this world that will produce a genuine sense of satisfaction, purpose and significance for your life apart from embracing the purposes and objectives of Jesus Christ.

No matter how many sermons you hear, no matter how many books you read or seminars you attend, apart from surrendering your life to Jesus Christ at the level of your will, you cannot experience lasting change in your life. Jesus alone is the source of your transformation. You cannot walk with Jesus and remain as you are. To experience Jesus Christ is to experience change!

For some of you it is extremely difficult to visualize significant changes occurring in your life. Through the years you have become so conditioned by failure that you no longer believe in the possibility that your life or circumstances can be different. You have experienced so little progress in your struggle to overcome the issues in your life that you have simply given up hope. My prayer is that the words of this book will serve as a constant reminder to you that—no matter how hopeless or powerless you may feel, no matter how often you may have failed in the past, no matter what the depth of your disappointment or frustration—the truth is: you can experience profound changes both in your personal life and in your circumstances. The choice is yours.

Notes

Chapter 1: Making Right Choices
[1]Ben Carson and Cecil Murphey, *Gifted Hands* (Grand Rapids, Mich.: Zondervan, 1990), pp. 56-59.

Chapter 2: It's Not My Fault!
[1]Stuart Goldman, "The Menendez Trial: Murder as Therapy," *National Review,* November 29, 1993, p. 44.
[2]Bill Clinton, quoted in Margaret Carlson, "Our Nattering Nabobs," *Time,* December 21, 1998, p. 30.
[3]Gregory Sophfronia and Scott Adam Cohan, "Black Rage Defense," *Time,* June 6, 1994, p. 31.
[4]Michael Liimatta, "Understanding Chemical Dependency," seminar notes, 1993, p. 41.

Chapter 3: Why Is It So Hard to Do the Right Thing?
[1]Knofel Staton, *Check Your Character* (Cincinnati: New Life Books, 1981), pp. 78-79.
[2]Charles Colson, *The Body* (Dallas, Tex.: Word, 1992), pp. 187-88.

Chapter 4: What You See Is Usually What You Get
[1]Dr. Clinton E. Arnold, "Three Views on Spiritual Warfare: Satan's Main Agenda," *Biola Connections Magazine,* winter 2002, p. 16.

Chapter 5: Consider It All Joy
[1]The Taylors' story is adapted from David Boehi, *I Still Do* (Nashville: Broadman & Holman, 2000), pp. 13-15.
[2]Ibid., p. 21.
[3]"Nelson Mandela," in *Great People of the 20th Century* (New York: Time Books, 1996), p. 56.

Chapter 6: Let the Walls Come Down!
[1]Dr. Neil T. Anderson, *Victory over the Darkness* (Ventura, Calif.: Regal, 1990), pp. 160, 164.

[2]Ibid., p. 128.
[3]Ibid., pp. 159-62, 168.
[4]Ibid., p. 161.

Chapter 7: It's All in the Mind
[1]Tom Dowling, *Coach: A Season with Lombardi* (New York: W. W. Norton, 1970).
[2]Randall Balmer, "Still Wrestling with the Devil," *Christianity Today,* March 2, 1998, p. 30.

Chapter 8: You Are More Than What You Have Become
[1]*The Lion King* (Burbank, Calif.: Walt Disney Home Video, 1995), videorecording.
[2]Charles R. Swindoll, *Living Above the Level of Mediocrity* (Dallas, Tex.: Word, 1987), p. 19.
[3]*The Complete Christian Dictionary for Home and School,* ed. All Nations Literature staff (Ventura, Calif.: Gospel Light, 1992), p. 740.
[4]*Lion King.*

Chapter 10: Hey God, Can You Hook Me Up?
[1]Curtis C. Mitchell, *Praying Jesus' Way* (Old Tappan, N.J.: Revell, 1977), pp. 95-113, 145-51.
[2]Ibid., p. 102.
[3]Henry T. Blackaby and Claude V. King, *Experiencing God* (Nashville: Broadman & Holman, 1994), p. 60.

Chapter 11: Someone Help Me, Please
[1]*Star Wars* (Beverly Hills, Calif.: 20th Century Fox, 1977), videorecording.
[2]Charles R. Swindoll, *Growing Deep in the Christian Life* (Grand Rapids, Mich.: Zondervan, 1995), pp. 76-77.
[3]Bill Bright, message to Campus Crusade for Christ national staff, Campus Crusade for Christ International Headquarters, San Bernardino, Calif., 1990.
[4]Crawford W. Loritts Jr., *A Passionate Commitment* (Chicago: Moody Press, 1989), pp. 102-3.

Acknowledgments

Cindy Bunch—my editor, who believed in this book project from the start. You are so pleasant to work with. Thanks, Cindy.

Kenneth Causey—my brother, friend and partner in ministry. Thanks for taking time to read the early versions of this manuscript. Your suggestions were valuable.

Donna Causey—Thanks, Sweetheart, for believing in me. Your input, keen insight and countless hours poring over the pages of this book made the difference.

Those who encouraged me to go for it:

Dr. Crawford Loritts, Jr.
Rev. Kelvin Lewis
Lisa Benton
Gary Stanley

I appreciate you!